A Publication Sponsored by the W.K. Kellogg Foundation

The W.K. Kellogg Foundation was founded in 1930 with a clear mission: "To help people help themselves through the practical application of knowledge and resources to improve their quality of life and that of future generations." The private foundation that began funding programs to meet the health and educational needs of Michigan children has grown to a position of national and international prominence for its assistance to communities in the United States, Latin America, the Caribbean, and southern Africa. Today the W.K. Kellogg Foundation is one of the largest philanthropic organizations in the world.

As a private grantmaking institution, the Kellogg Foundation provides seed money to nonprofit organizations and institutions that have identified problems and designed constructive action programs aimed at solutions. Most grants are awarded in the areas of higher education; youth development; leadership, philanthropy, and volunteerism; comprehensive health care systems; and rural development.

Building Partnerships

Ronald W. Richards, editor

· ·

Foreword by
William C. Richardson

Building Partnerships

. . . .

Educating Health Professionals for the Communities They Serve

Jossey-Bass Publishers
San Francisco

A Publication of the W.K. Kellogg Foundation

Substantial discounts on bulk quantities of Jossey-Bass books are available to corporations, professional associations, and other organizations. For details and discount information, contact the special sales department at Jossey-Bass Inc., Publishers. (415) 433–1740; Fax (800) 605–2665.

For sales outside the United States, please contact your local Simon & Schuster International Office.

 Manufactured in the United States of America on Lyons Falls Pathfinder Trade-book. This paper is acid-free and 100 percent totally chlorine-free.

Library of Congress Cataloging-in-Publication Data

Building partnerships : educating health professionals for the
  communities they serve / Ronald W. Richards, editor.
      p.   cm.—(The Jossey-Bass health series)
    Includes bibliographical references and index.
    ISBN 0-7879-0150-4 (alk. paper)
      1. Medical education policy—United States.   2. Primary care
  (Medicine)—Study and teaching—United States.   3. Community health
  services—Study and teaching—United States.   I. Richards, R.
  (Ronald)   II. Series.
  R743.B85   1996
  610'.71'173—dc20   95-9652
                                                                                CIP

HB Printing   10 9 8 7 6 5 4 3 2 1   FIRST EDITION

Contents

. . . .

Foreword

• •

From 1992 through 1994, health care reform was a hotly debated topic in Congress. Since that time, the literature has been full of attempts to explain why no major policy change resulted from the debate. Some interpretations express satisfaction with the legislative outcome—or lack of it. Others regret the absence of comprehensive health system reform. In either case, the problems that brought health reform to the forefront of public awareness—access to and availability of health care, the cost of care, and the need for more primary care and a system that delivers it—are still with us.

In the United States, foundations are often the channels for new approaches to complex problems. These uniquely American institutions—few other countries have philanthropic institutions protected, as these are, from taxation, so that they may do good for society—are independent of the democratic push and pull of the myriad interests that craft legislation in our country. In part because of their protected status, foundations are, in my mind, charged with doing three things: helping to define and provide facts about some of society's most important issues, establishing models for solving those important problems, and communicating widely what is learned in the process.

The W.K. Kellogg Foundation has been concerned with the health challenges facing people since its inception in 1930. The organization that began with modest funding primarily focused on children's health and education has expanded to one of the largest foundations in the world, with a wide range of funding interests related to pressing social issues. As the problems of people have become more complex, the projects selected for funding have necessarily become more innovative and more comprehensive. The Kellogg Foundation's philosophical commitment to seeking solutions in areas such as health rests on the belief that, if given the tools, individuals and communities will make changes for the better and on the conviction that, in the words of founder W.K. Kellogg, "education offers the greatest opportunity for really improving one generation over another."

It is often said at the Kellogg Foundation, "We *know* better than we do." Such is certainly the case in health professions education. We know how to graduate more and better-prepared doctors, nurses, and other health professionals to work together in teams. We know how to educate health professionals in more cost-effective ways in urban and rural communities. We *do* know better than we do. And in 1991, the Kellogg Foundation funded a seven-site initiative focusing on a new approach to health professions education to demonstrate ways to begin "doing."

Community Partnerships with Health Professions Education, a five-year initiative funded by $47.5 million in grants from the W.K. Kellogg Foundation, created seven linkages between communities and educational institutions to train health professionals. Through this initiative, hundreds of students—medical, nursing, physician assistant, social work, dental, allied health, and other health professions students—are today working and learning together in teams. The lessons being learned in these partnerships are the subject of this volume.

Building Partnerships: Educating Health Professionals for the Communities They Serve is intended to offer assistance to those who will develop alternative approaches to achieving the same goal—a workforce of health professionals that meets the needs of people. Rather than promote a single solution, this book is written in the hope that many solutions will be developed, encouraging the many ways in which health professions education systems can, and should, be adapted to increase their relevance to the needs of people.

August 1995   WILLIAM C. RICHARDSON
Battle Creek, Michigan
President and Chief Executive Officer
W.K. Kellogg Foundation

Preface

During a typically hot and sticky Washington, D.C., day late in July 1994, I was part of a presentation in the Russell Senate Office Building on the topic of health delivery system changes. During my years of observing the deliberations about health care reform in the United States, I had attended similar sessions on Capitol Hill in similar quarters. In this room, as in many of the others, high marble columns held up an ornate ceiling. The room was packed with policy makers and policy influencers of one sort or another. Representatives of various health professions education and health care organizations recounted statistics about workforce needs, demands for health care, the costs of health care, and various definitions of primary health care. No one in the room spoke about the communities across the country affected by these issues or about the people who lived in them. And yet I found my thoughts turning to the community people I had come to know in my role as program director for the Kellogg Foundation's Community Partnerships with Health Professions Education initiative—people who, whether the experts in that room recognized it or not, were actively engaged in educating future health professionals.

I thought of Sara Lee Neal, a longtime community leader from the small town of Rainelle, West Virginia. As chairperson of the joint governing board of West Virginia's Partnership effort, she had recounted to a state legislative body in January 1994 that her role in educating doctors and nurses for her rural town was the most important enterprise she had ever undertaken. As she explained, "In the grand scheme of this world, to truly make a difference is a blessing. We've made life better for folks who never dreamed to even ask for better hearts, better teeth, healthier children. The Kellogg initiative has given hope to populations who were drowning in resignation."

I wondered how Sara Lee Neal would react to one of the presentations I was hearing on that hot July day—a presentation about how 1982 workforce projections had accurately predicted the shortage of primary care health professionals. As she knew only too well, there was already a shortage of health professionals in Rainelle in 1982, and there is still a shortage today.

As I continued to listen to presentations, one speaker noted that primary care residency positions in the United States were being filled to a greater extent than in past years. He made the point that, if left alone, graduates of medical schools would eventually choose primary care specialties in greater numbers. I could not help thinking of Wanda Vaughn of Rogersville, Tennessee. As chairperson of the board of the small hospital in her town, she could not find doctors or nurses to staff it. And I remembered the man from Houghton Lake, Michigan, who, after listening to an explanation of the differences between primary care physicians and others, remarked, "I don't much care about what is or is not a primary care doctor. I don't much care functionally what they do or don't do. We don't have a doctor of any kind. I invite all of you to come with me to my county and see if it matters to the people there how you define it."

In Washington, our presenters were talking about geographic and specialty maldistribution of physicians. Nurses were not mentioned. Later, when a nurse practitioner colleague wondered aloud, "Why, again, are there no nurses making presentations?" I remembered a man from a small town of less than 3,500 people who declared, "My doctor is a nurse." He knew full well what he had said, and he meant every word of it.

The meeting in the Russell Senate Office Building went on, as did the many meetings that came before it and the many that would follow. At the center of this meeting, as at so many others, were the questions and the figures that fuel the fires of policy making: What is the problem? What is the solution? How much will that solution cost? In this country, we spend an average of $179,000 a year to educate each physician in postgraduate training. I do not doubt the good intentions of our policy makers and the necessity of focusing on global statements of issues at the federal level. I understand also the importance for lobbyists to put forward their best case and to examine issues in relation to the interests of their constituents. But those who speak loudest often have the most to lose. And as I listened to the speeches on Capitol Hill, I continued to wonder, *Who lobbies for people in communities?*

A recent report from the Alliance for Health Reform (1994) stated that we spend an estimated $6 billion in federal money alone on the education of medical specialists but only $56 million to promote the education of primary care practitioners. The gap between what people want and how public money is expended for health professions training is at the root of the primary health care crisis. The problem, however, is not a new one.

In the 1970s, geographical and specialty maldistribution were considered key to the lack of available primary care. The Alma Ata Declaration of 1978 established the commonality of worldwide concern for the need for primary care. In the following year, the international Network of Community-Oriented Education Institutions for Health Sciences was established to encourage the relevance of health personnel education to the needs of communities. Yet in 1988, the World Federation for Medical Education issued the Edinburgh Declaration, stating, "The aim of medical education is to produce doctors who will promote the health of all people, and that aim is not being realized in many places despite the enormous progress that has been made during this century in the biomedical sciences" (p. 8).

Private foundations have responded to the need for more primary care practitioners in a variety of innovative ways. The Pew Charitable Trusts and the Robert Wood Johnson Foundation in particular have focused interest and resources on addressing this need. The Pew Health Professions Commission (1991), for instance, confirmed that health professions education was out of step with public need. Commissions since have worked with federal, state, institutional, and professional associations to address workforce reform. The Robert Wood Johnson Foundation Generalist Physician Initiative is another example of an effort to seek institutional and market changes to expand the availability of primary care physicians.

Today all medical, nursing, and other health professions education institutions face the challenge of increasing the number of suitably prepared primary care practitioners. Adapting new selection criteria and curricula and identifying role models for primary care practitioners may contribute to reversing the decline in the number of graduates choosing primary health care. But even with these changes, most medical and nursing schools continue to focus on hospital preparation. If a shift from specialty care to primary care is to be accomplished, a transition from hospital-based education to education that incorporates the community perspective must precede it. Such a shift calls for a new mindset in health professions education—a redirection in the ways doctors, nurses, and other health professionals learn their craft.

Building Partnerships: Educating Health Professionals for the Communities They Serve is divided into eleven chapters. Chapter One summarizes information from consumer polls, devoting particular attention to a poll commissioned by the Kellogg Foundation in the spring of 1994. That poll—"What the Public Values in Its Health Care System"—provided valuable information about how people in this country feel about the health care currently available and how it does or does not meet their needs. Chapter Two looks at the gap between the culture of communities and the culture of academe and identifies the Community Partnerships model as one method of bridging the two. In Chapter Three, Rebecca C. Henry provides a description of each project and an update on the seven partnerships through their third year of funding.

In Chapter Four, the role of public policy in creating the current systems of health professions education, and in supporting change, is addressed in light of the experience of the seven Community Partnerships. Chapters Five, Six, and Seven describe the linchpins of the Community Partnerships model—academic health centers, community, and the new linking structures that bridge them. In Chapter Five, the history, nature, and organizational characteristics of academic health centers are examined. Bruce Behringer and I address the structure and dynamics of communities—their nature, leadership, and modes of participation—in Chapter Six. In Chapter Seven, Patricia Maguire Meservey and I consider the many challenges incumbent in creating viable linking organizations to connect academic institutions and communities.

Henry A. Foley expands on the interplay between the economics of health care and the education of providers in Chapter Eight. Rebecca C. Henry describes the role evaluation can play in the change process in Chapter Nine. In Chapter Ten, Patricia T. Castiglia examines the role of multidisciplinary education—training doctors, nurses, and other health professionals together—in redirecting health professions education toward primary care. And in the final chapter, the role of leaders and leadership in initiating and sustaining change is the subject.

In my view, professionals have lost some perspective on their social contract. The expertise of professionals helps maintain or restore health, design buildings and bridges, and apply the rule of law in mediating disputes and striving for justice. In return for these contributions to society, professionals are granted certain privileges. But when professionals lose sight of their accountability to communities as part of this arrangement, the distance between the two parties grows. Recent steps have been taken to turn around this gap between communities and the institutions of professionals. As developing legislation around health care in the United States has declared with appropriate timidity, "Enough."

From all parts of our society, we now proclaim the need for more primary health care and more suitably educated primary care practitioners to deliver it. In the United States of the 1990s, policy change will contribute to reshaping health professions education. But policy development, although it begins locally, moves back and forth through various democratic processes to effect change at state and federal levels. Built into the U.S. character (and thus into this country's systems) is an independent nature and a general distrust of government intervention. Congress, by its very nature, represents voters and interest groups and tends to compromise away many aspects of proposed programs. Policy making at the state level is no different. Innovative programs and new systems seldom flow from government, and policy change is a long and winding process.

By contrast, the Community Partnerships initiative is about the creation of academic, nonhospital, community health systems shaped in seven different ways by people and institutions at the local level. There are lessons to be learned from this initiative and new programs that must be created—many of them quite different from the Community Partnerships initiative—to prepare health professionals to meet the needs of people in communities. Experts from multiple segments of our society—individuals from academe, neighborhoods, clinics, schools, human service agencies, and private medical practices—all need to participate to effect lasting change. As one schoolteacher from Boston explained, "I want to be involved in educating doctors and nurses so they get it right!" So it should be for all of us.

August 1995   RONALD W. RICHARDS
                                                Battle Creek, Michigan

Acknowledgments

• •

There would be no book without the seven Community Partnerships—the seven unique combinations of community and academe that are developing and implementing models to redirect the education of health professionals toward multidisciplinary primary health care. There would be nothing to write about if it were not for the leadership evidenced in each of these projects—from academe, the community, and the new organizations that link these two together. In striving for something different—something better—the communities, academe, and the leadership of the Community Partnerships are taking many risks. This book is a testimony to the achievements of these extraordinary people, and it is for them. Five individuals have contributed chapters to this book as well. All of them are intimately involved with the Community Partnerships initiative and thus are able to provide in-depth reflection on their subjects. My thanks to each of them for their important contributions.

The Kellogg Foundation's role has been to provide funding for communities and universities to join together to achieve their own intentions for health professions educational reform. The Foundation's tasks could not have been accomplished without the contributions and regular critiques of my colleagues in health programming and communications at the Kellogg Foundation. They have helped to shape this initiative and have given me new experiences and insights. In addition, the observations of the Cluster Evaluation Team are woven throughout. My thanks also to Robert Bridgham and Marla Salmon for their comments.

Just as there would be no book without the Community Partnerships and the Kellogg Foundation, neither would there be one without the editorial assistance of Mary Cohen. She has interpreted, critiqued, rewritten, and generally prodded all of us. She has a most remarkable way of saying what needs to be said without offending. And she understands what the Community Partnerships initiative is all about. Her intellectual capacity is seen in every encounter. For all of this and more, my appreciation goes to Mary Cohen.

What one sees and how one interprets what is seen is obviously a function of many things. For me, weaving together this interim story of the Community Partnerships initiative has been an experience of trying to discover what I have seen and why I have seen it. My capacity to see and to interpret—flawed as it is and always will be—has been influenced by the caring people of communities, academe, and the Community Partnerships. I will forever be grateful for such insights.

Perhaps my capacity to see and interpret has been, more than anything, a function of past experiences. For most of these, my family has been more important than anything else, for they have prepared me to feel and experience that which might have been lost. Grandparents, parents, wife, and daughters have all been there with a challenge, a question, a point of view—frequently different than my own. I remember listening, as a youngster, as the challenges flowed back and forth across the kitchen table. In later years, when I made the transition from child observer to father, I was energized by the differing viewpoints of my daughters, Lisa and Suzy, and my wife, Ann. The influence of such exchanges on what I see and feel and on how I interpret can be found only slightly below the surface of this book. They will be with me forever. To my family, I extend a very special thank-you.

The Editor

· ·

RONALD W. RICHARDS is a program director at the W.K. Kellogg Foundation of Battle Creek, Michigan, where he is responsible for the Community Partnerships with Health Professions Education initiative. During his tenure with the Foundation, Richards has also headed program evaluation and been director of the Kellogg International Leadership Program.

Prior to joining the Kellogg Foundation, Richards served as professor of medical education, professor of education, and director of the Center for Educational Development (now the Department of Medical Education) at the University of Illinois, Chicago. His chief interests have been with reform processes in medical education, curriculum development, and primary care education. Richards was the founding director of Michigan State University's Upper Peninsula Medical Education Program. He also served as principal investigator on a World Health Organization–sponsored study of ten primary care–oriented medical schools in nine countries. In recognition of his work, he received that organization's award for contributions toward the goal of "Health for All." In addition, Richards has served as an educational consultant in more than fifteen countries.

Richards received his bachelor's degree in political science and economics from Miami University in Oxford, Ohio. He received his master's degree in social science education and his doctorate in higher education and organizational theory from Michigan State University in Lansing, Michigan.

The Contributors

BRUCE BEHRINGER is executive director of the Office of Rural and Community Health at East Tennessee State University in Johnson City. A graduate of Pennsylvania State University (B.S., 1972) and the University of North Carolina School of Public Health (M.P.H., 1978), Behringer was the executive director of the Virginia Primary Care Association from 1984 through 1992.

PATRICIA T. CASTIGLIA is dean and professor of the College of Nursing and Allied Health at the University of Texas, El Paso. A graduate of St. Vincent's Hospital in New York City (1955), Castiglia received her bachelor of science degree (1962), master's degree (1965), and doctorate from the State University of New York, Buffalo (1976). Castiglia was formerly the associate dean for Graduate Nurse Education at the State University of New York, Buffalo.

HENRY A. FOLEY was the first director of Ke Ola O Hawai'i, Inc., in Honolulu. He received his doctorate from Harvard University (1973) and completed the Harvard Executive Health Policy Program (1977). Prior to assuming his role as project director, Foley was administrator of the Health Resources Administration (1977–1980) and director of Behavioral Health Services for the Hawaii Department of Health.

REBECCA C. HENRY is project director for Cluster Evaluation of the Community Partnerships with Health Professions Education initiative in the Office of Medical Education, Research, and Development at Michigan State University in Lansing. Henry is a graduate of Denison University (B.S., 1974), Western Michigan University (M.A. in psychology, 1976), and Michigan State University (Ph.D., 1979). In addition to her academic work, Henry serves as a consultant to numerous health and educational organizations.

PATRICIA MAGUIRE MESERVEY is executive director of the Center for Community Health Education, Research, and Service (CCHERS) in Boston. In addition to her role in CCHERS, Meservey is an associate professor in the College of Nursing at Northeastern University. Meservey took her bachelor's (1976) and master's (1977) degrees in nursing from Boston University and her doctorate (1988) in higher education administration from Boston College.

• •

Primary Health Care
What the Public Wants

Ronald W. Richards

Some years ago in a small, rural town in the dead of winter, a few local people gathered to discuss the shortage of health professionals in their area. The snow swirled around outside the window of the coffee shop as they talked. "We can't seem to get doctors or nurses to come here," one man said. "When they have paid back their federal government scholarship, they leave . . . just about the time they know enough to do us some good." The state's medical and nursing schools, he added, had not been responsive to their plight.

Later a medical school dean was asked about the health care needs of this small community. "Look," he said, "I know we need to be more responsive. I know we need more primary care faculty role models to teach and influence our students. I know our curriculum needs to be adapted to preparing students for careers in these areas. But when I'm faced with recruiting physicians, I'll take a procedure-oriented specialist—a thoracic surgeon or an ophthalmologist—over a family physician every time. That's where the money is. That's the kind of clinical faculty member who will contribute the most to the medical school's bottom line."

In the United States, what citizens say they need and want in health care is a far cry from what they receive. Whether people are in urban or rural communities, in close proximity to medical facilities or miles away from the nearest clinic, the things they value and desire in health care are very different from the beliefs that shape health professions institutions and the training they structure. To understand the philosophical underpinnings of the Community Partnerships model and to appreciate the lessons learned in bringing it to life, this gap—the breadth and depth of it—must be examined closely.

Discovering What the Public Wants

Individual stories may convey a disturbing picture of the discrepancy between the needs of people and the priorities of health professions education today. But the results of a number of national opinion surveys provide a larger context for the flaws that stories often highlight, as well as more information on which to base analysis of the current system. Although few polls target people's attitudes and beliefs about health and medical care exclusively, the climate for sampling and examining public opinion related to health care has never been more favorable.

The U.S. public might claim to have been polled to death in an effort to gauge the strength of its collective will for health reform. In a sixteen-month period, Harvard health policy expert Robert Blendon and his colleagues (Blendon, Brodie, Hyams, and Benson, 1994) identified forty-four national polls that attempted to determine where the public stood on health reform options. Although Blendon and others who study public opinion polling continually emphasize that a poll is only a "snapshot"—a single reaction at one point in time—national surveys and polls that seek to capture public sentiment have come to play an increasingly important role in the development of policy issues and options.

Pollster Daniel Yankelovich (1992) describes the wider context in which any poll needs to be considered. Public opinion, he explains, unfolds over a long period of time—many years, in fact—in a series of predictable stages. From the early days of dawning awareness about a problem until such time (if ever) that the public morally and intellectually renders its judgment, seven distinct stages must occur.

In stages one and two, awareness of a problem or need leads to urgency. As the cry for change grows more compelling, choices emerge and policy options are developed, marking stage three. Resistance rears its ugly head in stage four—resistance to the costs and trade-offs implicit in policy change. Yankelovich calls this the "wishful thinking" phase—a time when the public reacts negatively to policy changes it did not help craft and resists change in general when faced with the costs and/or limitations required by any new policy. Following this initial resistance, the public begins to seriously weigh options during stage five. In stage six, he says, the public takes a stand intellectually. Only when these six critical steps are completed are people ready and willing to embrace change—the "public judgment" of stage seven.

The failure of health policy reform in 1994 is an example of this seven-phase process in its first four stages. Beginning with the 1992 election, poll after poll identified health system reform as an important issue (Blendon, Brodie, Hyams, and Benson, 1994). It moved from third on the list of major concerns during the 1992 presidential campaign to second by the time President Clinton took office. Over the next sixteen months, interest in the "health care crisis," as it was termed by the media, remained prominent in surveys, peaking in the spring of 1993. In response to this level of concern, policy makers crafted legislation to address it, offering the choices Yankelovich identifies as characteristic of stage three. But by the summer of 1994, it became clear that the growing urgency that policy makers interpreted as a ringing mandate for change had, as yet, several evolutionary stages to complete. Health reform sputtered in the hands of an ambivalent Congress in the summer session, and it died by fall.

Not surprisingly, Yankelovich would say. Stages five through seven were still to be completed. In fact, Yankelovich had predicted two years earlier the stalling of health reform in 1994. He suggested that policy makers and others were already misreading the signs of public will and exaggerating the maturity of public opinion on the subject: "The health care issue hasn't yet reached Stage 4 among the broad public" (1992, p. 108).

If public opinion and the polls we use to measure it are so easily misinterpreted, why do we give them so much credence? One answer may lie in examining the American character and the systems created by it. In numerous articles, Philip Lee, formerly of the Institute for Health Policy Studies at the University of California School of Medicine in San Francisco and more recently assistant secretary of the U.S. Department of Health and Human Services, has described the independence of the American character as a crucial dimension in the development of public policy (see, for example, Lee and Brindis, 1990). The uneasy relationship between government and the private sector, he suggests, is a tangible reflection of that independent character. We in this country harbor the belief that the best solutions are private ones, that centralized government is prone to excess, and that incremental change is somehow less suspect than sweeping change. These beliefs set up a natural resistance to policy change, however needed (and at times demanded) it may be. Those who would shape policy responsive to the needs of Americans must do so mindful of the explosive minefield this independent character can represent.

Any reform of U.S. systems is difficult, and health care reform is no exception. Special-interest groups, poor articulation of the issues by the Clinton administration, and faulty media strategies have all been suggested as reasons for the demise of federal health care reform. But as Yankelovich points out, the public has yet to reach clarity about what it wants. And even when that is decided, the changes will take not one but several congressional sessions to achieve.

If resistance is a natural state, as Lee suggests, then measuring public opinion becomes one way of understanding—and anticipating—resistance to policy change across a diverse, complex country.

Polling has its limitations, of course. As critics often note, it is not only what you ask in a survey but how you ask, when you ask, and to some extent why you ask that shape what you learn. But surveys and polls examined within the context of time and place, and with a realistic view of their limitations, can chart the progress of public opinion and attitudes toward current systems. For those seeking to identify and support what people want in health care, sampling public opinion is one instructive form of measurement.

What the Public Wants in Health Care

In the spring of 1994, the Kellogg Foundation sponsored a bipartisan national survey of the nation's health care consumers to learn what people want in their health care systems. Republican pollster Vince Breglio, director of polling for the 1988 Bush/Quayle ticket, paired with Democrat Celinda Lake, whose former firm directed polling for the 1992 Clinton/Gore campaign, to measure public attitudes about health care, health care providers, and the delivery of care in local communities.

The comments and preferences of the 1,000 registered voters who participated in this national survey echoed the results of a series of Kellogg Foundation–sponsored focus groups conducted a few months earlier. Focus group participants at each of five sites (Atlanta, Georgia; Boston, Massachusetts; Charleston, West Virginia; El Paso, Texas; and Muskegon, Michigan) talked freely about their experiences with health care professionals and systems. The goal of these sessions was not only to explore public attitudes but also to assess participants' understanding of commonly used terms and policy concepts critical to the health reform debate.

In the course of the focus groups, facilitators learned that many of the words used to describe or define health care were confusing and little understood. Terms such as "primary care," "health care," "preventive care," "medical care," and "health care provider" had multiple—often conflicting—meanings to focus group participants.

For example, many thought "health care provider" or "primary care provider" meant "health insurance provider." Specific names for types of health professionals also puzzled participants. The roles and qualifications of the "physician assistant" and "nurse practitioner," for instance, were poorly understood except by those who had received services from them. With the exception of "doctor" and "nurse," most of the titles used to describe health professionals— and the language employed to talk about health care—had little consistent meaning to participants.

In October 1993, the Kaiser/Harvard/PRSA Survey of Public Knowledge came to similar conclusions regarding public awareness and understanding of specific health policy terms (Blendon and Altman, 1993). When asked questions about their familiarity with terms related to proposed health policy reform, 19 percent said that they had never heard of HMOs, 36 percent said that they had never heard of managed care, and 54 percent said that they had never heard of managed competition.

Building on what was learned in the focus group sessions and in other samplings of public opinion, the Kellogg consumer survey was designed to avoid confusing terms, and it framed questions using simpler language than earlier surveys to gather information on public attitudes about health care. Since people in the focus groups had used the term "family doctor" to mean the doctor they saw on a regular basis, "primary care provider" or "family practitioner" became "family doctor" in the survey. In the same vein, "general practitioners," "nurse practitioners," and "physician assistants" were called "basic health care providers," and medical subspecialists such as "neurosurgeons" were called simply "medical specialists."

The clues to public attitudes and values that emerged, then, were not muddied by the complex micro-languages of medical systems and policy. In the context of other polls and opinion surveys, the Kellogg Foundation poll and the focus groups that helped shape it have expanded our understanding of what people seek from health providers—and how current systems and services help or hinder them in their search.

Information on the more intangible dimensions of health services is seldom sought in surveys and polls. Public opinion samplings by private interest groups and media have tended to focus on the "horse race" aspects of health reform: Whose plan has the edge? What are the prospects for this proposal? Would you support this legislator's idea for funding? Very little comment has been invited about what people want in health care. Yet when asked, as they were in the Kellogg Foundation survey, people tell us what they want and need quite succinctly. Some of the survey's findings are discussed in the paragraphs that follow.

Although an impressive majority (89 percent) of the 1,000 consumers polled in the Kellogg survey had some form of health coverage, a majority of that same 1,000 felt that the current health care system failed to meet the needs of most U.S. citizens. Six in ten poll participants indicated that the country was on the wrong track in health care. Although many were optimistic that the next generation would receive better health care, a solid majority (66 percent) thought that the existing systems did not meet the needs of most people.

In this respect, the results of the Kellogg poll jibe with other surveys. Analyzing polls commissioned by the *New York Times*, the *Los Angeles Times*, and ABC News/*Washington Post*, Blendon reported that concerns about affordability and security of coverage have shaped popular attitudes toward health care (Blendon, Brodie, Hyams, and Benson, 1994). The fear that coverage may not pay for needed medical expenses in the future affects our perceptions about health care today.

Focus group participants also spoke of gaps they perceived in current health care systems. Concerns about health care cost, security, access, and quality permeated the discussions. "Until recently, I had my own small business, so it was impossible for me to afford health care." "After I lost my last job, they offered me COBRA, but I can't afford that type of insurance. Now I don't have any." "I think that the more money you have in this country, the better health care is available to you, and that's unfortunate. I think it ought to be available to everyone." "I'm fifty-three years old. I've got no insurance—I've got to pay out of my pocket when something happens to me—and I don't have a job that's going to pay any insurance." "My mother was put on an oxygen machine a couple of years ago. That's about $350 to $400 a month."

Focus group comments about the health care system as a whole ranged from mixed—"It has some rough spots in it"—to very negative, depending on the individual's experience and needs. Although many felt that the resources for excellent care were available, most questioned their availability to all citizens. As one man stated, "The health care system in America is one of the worst when it comes to poor people and people of color."

Despite such criticism of the U.S. health care system, survey and focus group participants had a strikingly clear view of the characteristics they value in health care providers and services—and where they would like to see health care move in the future. The prevalence of several key themes in poll and focus group responses illustrates the richness of the consumer's vision.

"Mutual Trust and Respect"

When asked to rate the importance of assorted features of health care, Kellogg poll respondents gave top grades to "a feeling of mutual trust between doctor and patient" and "respect from a doctor." Ninety-three percent of survey participants said "mutual trust" was either extremely important or very important; 89 percent ranked "respect" of similar importance. More than any other aspects of service, participants in every age, gender, political, educational, and racial grouping identified these features as vitally important.

"A Doctor Who Knows My History"

Consumers indicated that, on the heels of mutual trust and respect between provider and patient, a doctor's knowledge of the patient and his or her family was crucial. Thirty-five percent rated this feature "extremely important"; 56 percent rated it "very important."

Focus group participants previewed the likely response to this item. Most indicated that a provider needed to be attuned to the patient, his or her family, and the patient's unique needs. As one man put it, "It all goes back to family doctors. . . . If you're black and have things like diabetes or heart disease in your family, it's extremely helpful to have care from someone who knows your history—whether that history is six months ago or two generations ago."

"Access to a Team of Health Professionals"

Eighty-five percent of poll respondents rated "access to a team of health professionals" as either "extremely important" or "very important." Four in ten of the consumers polled had been treated by someone other than a doctor when seeking care. Consumers reported treatment by nurses (55 percent), nurse practitioners (50 percent), and physician assistants (9 percent), with 85 percent of these saying they were either "satisfied" or "very satisfied" with the care they received.

"Access to Basic and Preventive Care"

"Access to preventive care like check-ups and X-rays" was rated "extremely important" by 23 percent of poll respondents and "very important" by 58 percent. "The availability of basic health care for things like flu and routine illnesses" also ranked relatively high in importance: 71 percent rated this feature either "extremely impor- tant" or "very important." Focus group participants were less famil- iar with preventive health care; in many cases, it was either not available or too expensive. But many recognized the value of pre- ventive care. As one person said, "People don't go when they should—to get a mammogram or Pap smear—because they can't afford it."

"More Doctors and Nurses to Provide Basic Health Care"

When asked to choose how the government should spend U.S. tax dollars earmarked for health professions training, a majority of consumers polled favored increasing support for the training of family doctors (55 percent), nurses (59 percent), and other basic health care providers (52 percent). Forty-six percent of those polled indicated that public support of the training of generalists should be equal to support for the training of specialists. Thirty-three percent indicated that support for generalist training should be double that of specialist training. Only a small percentage of consumers (10 percent) endorsed spending twice as much on the education and training of specialists.

"A Role for Communities"

Fifty-four percent of consumers felt that "communities having some say in how health care is delivered" was either "extremely important" or "very important," while another 26 percent indicated that this feature was "somewhat important." Fifty-one percent rated "access to a family doctor or nurse that reflects my culture and background" "extremely important" or "very important." Focus group participants also saw communities as key to appropriate health services delivery. "When I was a kid, the doctor lived in my community. We weren't rich or anything, but we had a doctor and dentist whose offices were in their homes right in our community. We don't have that anymore." "A person who isn't associated with your community is like someone speaking a foreign language. . . . That person can't communicate with you very well." "A community can tell you where it hurts—where the need is—faster than you can figure it out for yourself."

What the Public Wants: More Primary Care

The above six themes, identified in poll and focus group responses, essentially describe the features of good primary care. Although assorted definitions of the term *primary care* have been used and refined since its introduction in 1961, the Institute of Medicine's 1994 provisional definition encompasses earlier efforts and offers a broad, comprehensive vision of the concept: "Primary care is the provision of integrated, accessible health care services by clinicians who are accountable for addressing a large majority of personal health care needs, developing a sustained partnership with patients, and practicing in the context of family and community" (Donaldson, Yordy, and Vanselow, 1994, p. 9).

As report editors Molla Donaldson, Karl Yordy, and Neal Vanselow explain, the words so carefully chosen to build this definition address the multidimensional features of primary care services. "Integrated" speaks to a "seamless process of care" occurring in diverse settings and at varying levels throughout every stage of a patient's life. "Clinicians" are individuals with "a recognized scientific knowledge base" and the authority and responsibility for directing and delivering health care to meet patient needs. "Sustained partnership" refers to the relationship between patient and clinician—a relationship "predicated on the development of mutual trust, respect, and responsibility." The "context of family and community" addresses the need for care to reflect an understanding of the patient's family dynamics, living conditions, cultural background, and ethnic heritage (pp. 9–20).

What poll respondents and focus group participants described through stories, ratings, and comments is comprehensive primary care as the Institute of Medicine defines it. The care is patient-focused and built on respect and trust between patient and provider; services include sick care and preventive care; and care at all levels is delivered by professionals who understand the patient's history, family, and community.

What the Public Generally Gets

The features consumers identify as important—the same features that define primary care and the importance of primary care providers—may not be widely available in the health care systems of the future. The primary care that consumers say they want may not be possible, because the doctors and nurses and other professionals needed to deliver it may not exist. Quite simply, our current systems will not provide an adequate number of primary care providers to meet future demands.

The systems we have in place now will certainly provide more doctors. Jonathan Weiner (1994) of the Johns Hopkins School of Public Health predicts that the supply of physicians will exceed projected system needs by 30 percent in the year 2000. The Council on Graduate Medicine's more conservative estimate—a 25 percent increase in the physician-to-population ratio by 2020—is no less impressive (Cowill, 1994). But the bulk of these physicians are trained in hospital residency programs in large metropolitan areas. The projected oversupply of non–primary care specialists based on population need, Weiner notes, is double that of physicians in general.

We may have a great many doctors in this country—and in the next ten years a great many more—but the question remains: *Do we have the providers that people say they need and want to deliver the type of care they value?*

According to the numbers, we do not. The data of the Association of American Medical Colleges (AAMC), for example, show that the percentage of U.S. medical school seniors planning to enter primary care specialties fell from 37.3 percent in 1981 to a low of 14.6 percent in 1992 (Kassenbaum and Szenas, 1992). The percentage of U.S. medical school seniors planning careers in family practice has also decreased—from 17 percent in 1986 to 13.7 percent in 1989 (Association of American Medical Colleges, 1990). Although the 1994 figures from the AAMC show an improvement in this picture—22.8 percent of 1994 medical students are planning primary care careers—the numbers continue to fall short of the need. Even if the percentage of graduates choosing primary care rose to produce the recommended 50:50 balance between primary care and non–primary care specialties, it would be decades before the practice population of physicians was equally balanced (Politzer, Harris, Gaston, and Mullan, 1991).

From 1965 until 1989, while the number of neurologists grew fourfold, the number of pulmonary specialists grew fivefold, the number of cardiologists grew eightfold, and the number of radiation oncologists grew fiftyfold, the relative number of family practitioners, pediatricians, and internists combined decreased. In 1963, there were 36.8 family physicians per 100,000 Americans; by 1986, that figure had dropped to 22 per 100,000 (Garg, Boex, Davis, and Rodos, 1993). From 1989 to 1991, the number of U.S. medical graduates matched with positions by the National Residency Matching Program showed an overall decline of 19 percent in primary care.

Yet as the supply of primary care practitioners has ebbed, public expenditures supporting graduate medical education have grown significantly. In the academic year 1990–91, the public contributed more than $97,000 per medical resident through federal and state funding sources. In other words, the medical education system that produces specialists to generalists at a ratio of 2:1 has little financial incentive to change.

The Difference Between What People Want and What They Get

The data suggest that there is a disconnect between the health care system people want and the one public dollars support through the training of health professionals. In both urban and rural America, the need for providers to deliver basic health care continues unabated. And in large metropolitan areas, the glut of narrowly focused specialty physicians continues to grow in excess of the needs of local people and their communities.

While people say that they want providers who deliver needed services in the context of their families and communities, most physicians and nurses continue to train in tertiary care hospitals—culturally removed from people, communities, and all but the effects of community problems. While people say that they want routine sick and preventive care, our health professionals spend their days and nights in high-tech settings learning on the sickest of the sick. While people say that they want a qualified team of providers working together to meet their needs, doctors continue to train only with doctors, nurses with nurses, social workers with social workers, and so on. More providers, trained in the way providers have been trained for the last thirty years, whatever their specialty, will not give people what they say that they want in health care. Some fundamental changes must occur.

Consideration of the outcomes of current training—the type and distribution of providers, where and what they practice—begins to identify the problems within our health professions education systems. But only by looking at how, where, and why we train providers the way we do—and comparing those forces with the needs and desires of the communities those providers must serve—will we really begin to grasp the scope of change that may be required to alter outcomes.

There is little argument that the United States has the most sophisticated technology and the best medical care in the world. But the people of our society have other needs as well. At one Community Partnership site, they tell of the time a mother and father carried their child to one of the Partnership's school-based clinics. The child was not ill, as it turned out; the child was dead. When clinic staff realized the situation, they explained to the parents that there was nothing they or anyone else could do for the little one. To the staff's surprise, the parents said that they knew the child was dead. They had come not for medical services but for the other services their friends and neighbors had said the clinic would provide—for understanding and emotional support, for kindness and caring. What this family wanted was not high-tech intervention but compassion.

The challenge of changing systems, changing paradigms, changing perspectives is always a daunting one. Change is a slow process, and all systems resist it. In the case of health systems, people seek more primary health care. But important issues—such as legal issues associated with the U.S. tort system, ethical concerns regarding access to and availability of end-of-life care, and the relative status of high-tech care versus basic primary care—remain. If health professions education is to prepare an adequate workforce to meet public needs in the decades to come, the desires and values of the people whom medical providers serve must be recognized and embraced. Perhaps the demands of our times—and the poignant, ongoing needs of our people—will provide the catalyst for change. And with that impetus, health professions leadership will rise to the challenge.

2

From Problems to Solutions

A Bridge Between Cultures

Ronald W. Richards

Teaching what people value in health care is not easy. Teaching budding health professionals the skills they need to develop relationships with patients based on trust and mutual respect is complex and time-consuming. Teaching nurses and doctors and public health professionals to listen and learn from people, and to involve communities in their care, stretches the limits of health professions education even further. Yet these are the features of health care people say that they value. These are the "intangibles" communities desire in their health systems. And these are the elements that people in Community Partnerships believe that they can help teach the next generation of health professionals.

Community representatives from the Transkei in South Africa and from Alabama, West Virginia, and Boston articulate the desire for patient-provider relationships based upon mutual respect. Indeed, for those receiving care, mutual respect is the *measure* of a patient-provider relationship. More than any other feature or commonality—more than similar ethnic background, race, employment, education, or community of origin—mutual respect between provider and patient builds a common ground. In Alabama, one rural community peopled by folks who are poor and predominantly black has a long-standing, productive collaboration with a professor of nursing at Auburn University. The professor does not live in the community, and she has little in common with its residents: she is white, well educated, and financially stable. But she does have an extraordinary working relationship with the people she serves. By her account and theirs, the relationship is based upon mutual respect that has developed and been tested over a long period of time.

Building a trusting relationship is difficult under any circumstances. Bridging the gap between the culture of academe, where health professionals are educated, and the culture of communities, where care is delivered, is additionally difficult. In an early phase of the Community Partnerships initiative, a series of seminars was conducted to explore the issue of linking academe with community. During the third seminar, a professor of family practice at a medical school exclaimed to the assembled group, "I'm afraid I'll go to the people of communities to collaborate only to discover that my expertise isn't needed." In response to that risky declaration of honesty, one community representative stood up in a far corner of the same room and answered, "Just trust us."

Community Partnerships communities have answered thus many times and in many ways. As part of the initiative, community health centers are becoming *academic* community health centers. At a forum in one small West Virginia town, the townspeople were asked if they realized that the program was primarily intended not to provide needed health care services but rather to educate a future generation of health professionals. Their responses made it clear that they understood, so they were asked a second question: "Why, then, are you involved?" The answer came immediately from a woman who described herself as "just a housewife": "We want to help teach students respect and trust and let them know there's more to their professions than earning high salaries in the suburbs. And we want to give the kids in our town an idea about going to college."

Whether people are bounded by the culture of communities or the culture of academe and hospitals, mutual respect and trust transcend the characteristics that divide us. At the level of human beings, to trust is in turn to be trusted. But academics and community people, patients and providers, live and work in different worlds. They are socialized and learn to survive in different cultures. Although they reside in relative proximity, the differences between their cultures are vast. The cultural experiences that divide academic institutions and communities may not be as obvious as those that separate Latin America from Midwestern America, or Capetown from Kialichia in South Africa. But the distinctive influences that shape the culture of communities and the culture of academic health centers are pervasive and far-reaching. In many ways, they transcend geopolitical boundaries. The differences between providers and communities of patients in West Virginia may be found not only in other U.S. communities but in Brazil, Zimbabwe, and Mexico.

Two Distinct Cultures

Communities have a culture unlike that of academe or any other organization. Henrie Treadwell (1994), in assessing the dynamics of the W.K. Kellogg Foundation's community-based approach to health programming, has suggested three tendencies that characterize communities and community leaders:

1. Communities and their leaders have a need for broad visions to be broken down into opportunities for mini-successes—to segment sweeping changes into more manageable tasks or actions that can address immediate barriers and be completed in succession.

2. Communities tend to frame problems differently than institutions or other organizations. Communities and their leaders do not typically describe problems in the abstract terms of health or clinical psychology. They define problems more concretely, because they see them from a different angle.

3. Finally, communities and their leaders are more often motivated by what they believe to be right than by what others
   think. That which they know is "real," based on their unique
   experiences and beliefs, drives their actions.

Communities have other distinctive characteristics as well.
Communities are dynamic and ever-changing, built on fluid
linkages that connect community members and groups to one
another. Although they often lack a formal organizational structure
and a strategic approach to process, communities are able to encompass relationships, history, and personal circumstances into their
problem-solving efforts. Community representatives often display
a humility and commitment to values uncommon in positions of
leadership. They see clearly that their role is to be accountable to
the people of their community, to work to increase people's control
over their lives. Yet communities are also involved in a series of
never-ending turf wars. Like universities and other organizations,
communities attempt to ensure survival by controlling their sources
of funds.

Academic health centers tend to be highly structured. A product
of university medical schools and the teaching hospitals where most
health professions training takes place, academic health centers
depend on formal organizational structures to define relationships
and dictate patterns of interaction. The hierarchy within academic
health centers is based on volume of resources. Individual departments often have the greatest influence on curriculum and student
time, because they control independent resources from research and
patient care services. Leaders in academic health centers, then,
often see themselves as accountable primarily to the goals and needs
of their individual departments.

Use of a strategic approach to problem solving is the norm in
these settings. Decisions are often made "by committee." But those
who are invited to participate in the process—the people who actually sit at the table—are subject to few influences outside of their

departments or practice settings. Strategy, then, may often be geared toward perpetuating the influence of the department or school rather than addressing a specific problem or need.

Communities and academic cultures are distinct and separate, but they also have some common tendencies. Competition for prestige and control of people and resources is not unique to academe, by any means. Community representatives—be they representatives of formal human service organizations, neighborhood block clubs, or public housing projects—compete for resources and control in ways remarkably similar to the ways departments jockey for position in academe and clinical service units in large hospitals struggle for prominence. Both the organizations of communities and those of academe engage in political sparring to reach win-win agreements (Baldridge and Deal, 1975). In these respects, academe and community are more the same than different.

There are people in communities and people inside of academe who want to build on these similarities—to collaborate to reduce the gap between what people want and what they get from professionals of all types. Reducing that gap depends upon an understanding by academe of community and an understanding by community of academe. It depends on a willingness of both parties to give to a common purpose in the short run for mutual benefit in the long run. To institutions and communities willing to risk this level of collaboration and understanding, the Community Partnerships with Health Professions Education initiative has been a unique opportunity.

The gap between the structures of communities and those of academic health centers can be bridged by people on both sides who are willing to check their biases and to seek to establish relationships based upon knowledge, understanding, and common purpose. But honesty and openness in the exchange of views between academics and communities are rare. In many ways, neither group seems to recognize the cultural discrepancies that impair interaction and mutual understanding. Often academics seem not to understand the discouraging effect of defining communities solely by their weakest links. Problems of drugs, gangs, domestic violence, teenage pregnancy, and infant mortality may constrain communities. But such challenges do not necessarily define their capacity. By the same token, community people seldom appreciate that an academic institution is not a single source of power but a connection of departments and faculties, each with a single piece of the university's resources. Community people and others outside academic institutions would be surprised to learn how little representatives of universities can deliver unilaterally—how little autonomy and independence they have.

The reasons for this type of misunderstanding, or lack of understanding, are many. Some can be linked to the natural barriers that separate those inside a system from those outside it. Some are rooted in the nature of our health care system and the way it is funded. (Chapter Eight considers these dimensions in depth.) But other reasons are more closely related to the nature of the relationship between professionals and society—in Hobbesian terms, the nature of the social contract.

Professions and professional education are caught in a "knowledge trap." In this trap, more emphasis is placed on acquiring a distinctive, ever-growing body of knowledge than on applying what has been learned to complex societal problems. In a book entitled *The Culture of Professionalism: The Middle Class and the Development of Higher Education in America*, Burton J. Bledstein (1976) makes this point very well. The authority of the professional, he states, rests in the ability to "release nature's potential and rearrange reality on scientific grounds." Professionals, he explains, acquire power through their control of "a magic circle of scientific knowledge which only the few specialized by training and indoctrination are privileged to enter" (p. 90). Such "magic circles" of knowledge are the basis both for the professions' contribution to society and for their avoidance of society's problems. Professionals, Bledstein argues, tend to look for problems that fit the "magic circle" of their own knowledge base. For attorneys, all of society's problems are legal ones. Among legislators, policy is the defining element of modern life. Each profession "rearranges reality," according to Bledstein, on the basis of its unique expertise.

But such an approach leaves many societal problems unattended. Says Donald Schön, "The crisis of confidence in the professions and perhaps also the decline in professional self image . . . hinges centrally on the question of professional knowledge. Is it sufficient to meet the societal demands which the professions have helped to create?" (1983, p. 13). The gap between what people want and what they get from professionals of all types is widening.

Creating a Bridge: The Community Partnerships with Health Professions Education Initiative

Simply put, the Community Partnerships with Health Professions Education (CP/HPE) initiative seeks to increase the number of suitably prepared primary care practitioners by reducing the gap between the culture of the community and the culture of academe and hospitals. The rationale for CP/HPE, in its most simplified form, is to create an organizational structure that links academic health centers and the community. Such a structure, in turn, creates an *academic community health system* made up of community health centers, school-based clinics, and other health and human service enterprises, and it changes the curricula of medicine, nursing, and other health professions schools by addressing the needs and desires of the community. In Community Partnerships sites, students in various health professions programs spend significant amounts of time learning together in out-of-hospital settings. Through this restructuring, health professions education begins to move from a culture of academe and hospitals to a culture of communities.

Easier said than done, of course. The dynamics of both communities and academic health centers, the difficulties of linking organizational structures and sharing (or relinquishing) power, the complexities of multidisciplinary education, the economic realities of health care today, the exigencies of institutional and public pol-icy—all these present formidable challenges, and each will be addressed in subsequent chapters of this volume. But for now, let us consider the major elements of the Community Partnerships model and how they support this shift of cultures.

At the heart of each Community Partnership is the formation of an academic, community-based primary health system. The com-mon mission of these seven newly formed organizations that bring community and academic health centers together is threefold: to educate health professions students in community settings, to pro-vide a base for the academic research of faculty, and to deliver much-needed primary care services to communities. Although the elements of individual partnerships vary, the common characteris-tics create a unique learning environment for students, faculty, and community members:

- *The systems are academic.* Each Community Partnership provides instruction and services and conducts compre-hensive, community-focused research.

- *The systems are community-based.* Each reflects new organizational partnerships between communities and academic institutions.

- *The systems have a primary care focus.* Community Part-nership systems strive to keep people healthy, attend the sick, and help patients and their families maintain dignity and control by delivering multidisciplinary, comprehensive primary care.

Academic, community-based primary care systems serve as the focal point for institutions and communities working together. They support shifts in the patterns of interaction and in the organizational structures of both the academic and community institutions they bring together. Just as health education institutions have much to share with communities, communities have much to teach developing health professionals and their faculty. Community Partnerships foster mutual respect between academic health centers and communities, joining the interests of both in a common goal.

Governance structures formalize the linkages these partnerships engender and create a new organizational force in the academic and larger community. Academic, community-based health systems are guided by boards with representation from the educational institutions providing students, the faculty teaching them, the community centers where services are delivered, and the consumers receiving the services. If a partnership meets the needs of all partners, a representative governance structure ensures that the partnership will be sustained.

Academic community health system boards engage in the planning and administration necessary to nurture Community Partnerships. These boards oversee the implementation of the model, track student involvement and consumer satisfaction, and address system policy needs. Boards also monitor the funding status of their systems and seek new, additional funds as needed to support sustainability of the systems beyond the Kellogg Foundation grant period.

The independent resources and financial health of the partnerships also serve to attract participants in academic health centers to shared, rather than fragmented, purposes. Existing funding streams tend to empower individual departments, their faculty, and students. Community Partnerships funding joins faculty and students across departments and provides an incentive for multidisciplinary collaboration within academic institutions and outside their walls.

Those who created CP/HPE never doubted the human calling that motivates most health professionals to serve. Academic health centers—the university medical centers that train our country's physicians, nurses, and other health professionals—will play a central role in helping to fashion solutions to society's health care crisis. Many health professionals see the need for change, and many want to make productive changes. Furthermore, academic health centers in general know that their future depends on redirecting their systems toward community responsiveness. Yet all are trapped in a bureaucratic and governmental status quo that makes the creation of alternatives very difficult.

Through Community Partnerships, selected institutions in seven sites throughout the United States have been assisted in creating new organizational structures in partnership with communities. The structures are designed to be far enough outside of the educational and health care status quo to be the basis for new primary health care–oriented funding patterns. The structures are governed and controlled by community/academic partnerships—linking organizations that support collaboration. In turn, these collaborative structures are responsible for creating a new kind of setting for the education of health professionals—an academic community health system.

Socialization in Health Professions Training

The centrality of these academic community health systems is based on the belief that the essence of health professions education is less a matter of knowledge acquisition and more a matter of socialization—that is, a function of what students experience, what they observe, and the nature of the setting in which all of this happens. The Community Partnerships' focus on creating alternative settings for student learning is predicated on the belief that the present choices of settings for health professions education are inadequate.

In the course of their training, most health professions students are based either in teaching hospitals and their affiliated clinics or, to a lesser extent, in practitioner settings for field experiences. Perhaps the most telling way academic health systems have structured health professions training is through allocation of student time to specific clinical experiences in a single practice setting. Hospital-based health professions education instructs students not only in *how* to practice medicine and nursing but *where* to practice. And physicians and nurses learn how to be health care professionals almost exclusively in acute care settings. Although many aspects of medical care are best taught in hospitals, that setting also limits students' opportunities for learning in many respects.

For instance, the tertiary care facilities in academic health centers serve a great percentage of high-risk patients with serious health problems. The availability and use of technology in these settings reflect the critical conditions of the patients. Certainly, the likelihood of aggressive intervention in caring for gravely ill patients is very high. Aggressive intervention saves lives in critical care situations.

The more serious the patient's problems, however, the more specialized the treatment needed. When a severely ill patient presents in the ER, the pediatrician calls in the pediatric neurologist or the internist looks to the pulmonary specialist. While the specialists' expertise and supporting technology are an integral part of the capacity of a tertiary care facility, the type of patients and the type of facility increase the likelihood that a specialist's care will be required. Education in such an environment is an education in high-technology specialist care.

Other unique features of hospital-based training—the language, attire, and customs—shape students as much as their clinical experiences. The hospital culture and its parameters—who addresses whom, for example, how, when, and why—are all part of the informal curriculum of hospital-based health professions training. In hospitals, medical students learn some of the patterns of interaction they carry with them throughout their careers; doctors interact with doctors, nurses with nurses, and interprofessional collaboration is limited at best. Students absorb the hospital hierarchy—its rewards and constraints—as readily as they absorb information about procedures and practices. They know who has the power to promote within academic health centers and what type of clinical interest will be recognized. They understand what skills are valued within the hospital culture and what areas of expertise are considered second-rate.

Hospital-based training also impacts how much students can learn about patients. In hospitals, patients seek care on the physician's "turf." What the provider learns about the patient is confined to examination and interview. Since students see their patients in isolation, they must accept the information they receive at face value. Medical students focus on each patient's symptoms, not on the conditions or circumstances that might have produced them. With little firsthand knowledge about a patient's community, the student health professional has only his or her life experiences— and the experience of faculty—to draw on when assessing a patient's needs. The student's family, school, and training background must guide his or her judgment. In the end, the student health professional's experiences are expanded only as far as the academic health center's walls will allow.

By confining most of students' clinical experiences to acute care settings, academic health centers send subtle (and not-so-subtle) messages to reinforce student perceptions about practice choices. Through hospital-based training, students may learn the following, for example: the business of medicine is intervening with very ill patients; there is a great deal to know, and specialists know "more" of what is important to know; cutting-edge, high-tech medicine is practiced in hospitals; research and scholarship are part of working in hospitals. In other words, hospitals are where you practice "real" medicine and "real" nursing.

Under these circumstances, health professions education promotes a mindset that affects students and graduates—a division between a high-quality academic world and a lower-quality practitioner world. The third setting, that of an *academic but nonhospital community health system,* is needed. The need for this new setting for education is not unlike the need that prompted the creation of teaching hospitals in the first place—a setting wherein the best of health care and research could be conducted and where students could be placed for their training.

Change from the Outside In

A second belief has significantly influenced the development of the Community Partnerships model: the belief that change in organizations happens from the outside in. No organization of professionals, however many of its members believe that change is necessary, is likely to willingly make radical adaptations in its structure and functions. Change in organizations more often occurs as a response to outside pressures. In medical schools, for example, departments of family practice were added in the 1970s because state legislators demanded them, not because faculties of medicine had decided that such organizational adaptation was desirable. Centers for continuing education have been established at universities more often because the incentive of tuition and registration income appeared than because the faculties decided that they should make their expertise more widely available to society. In most organizations, academic institutions among them, change comes in response to outside pressures.

Generally, the faculty members of academe are isolated from the outside world—the world upon which academe depends, ironically, for its students, research funds, and patient care dollars. By reducing this isolation, the community/academic linkages of the Community Partnerships bring the forces of the outside world to bear on health professions education. The stronger the forces from the outside world upon academe, the greater the likelihood of positive response from academic institutions. CP/HPE depends, in other words, on creating and harnessing outside forces to achieve change within health professions educational institutions.

Samuel W. Bloom (1988) has provided scholarly documentation for his assertion that "preparation of physicians to serve the changing health needs of the society is asserted repeatedly as the objective of medical education. But this manifest ideology of humanistic medicine is little more than a screen for the research mission which is the major concern of the institution's social structure. Education is secondary and essentially unchanging, even though brave ideological statements guide curriculum reforms that do little but mask the underlying reality" (p. 295).

Learning from the Partnerships

Community Partnerships provide a framework for health professions education to create a new social structure by linking with community and to redesign curriculum by changing the setting. CP/HPE involves seven such alternative organizational structures, each of which seeks to create an opportunity for a significant proportion of the education of health professionals to occur in out-of-hospital, community-linked experiences:

• In Georgia, the Morehouse School of Medicine, Georgia State University School of Nursing, and Clark Atlanta University's programs in social work and allied health have joined with five federally funded community health centers and the neighborhood councils representing the populations they serve to delivery primary care services in Atlanta and rural Georgia.

• In Massachusetts, Boston University's School of Medicine and Northeastern University's College of Nursing team with a network of community health centers and Boston's public health agency to involve all medical and nursing students in interdisciplinary team education at community sites.

• In Tennessee, East Tennessee State University Schools of Medicine, Nursing, and Public and Allied Health work with communities and local and state agencies to expand care and health services to rural community members.

- *In Texas*, the University of Texas at El Paso and Texas Tech University Health Sciences Center have joined with local consumers and providers to establish clinics in elementary schools, meeting the health needs of students and their families in remote, underserved areas.
- *In Hawaii*, the University of Hawaii Schools of Medicine, Nursing, Social Work, and Public Health link with clinics in Honolulu and rural Oahu to provide primary care services at community health centers and less traditional sites, such as local high schools.
- *In Michigan*, Michigan State University Colleges of Human Medicine, Osteopathic Medicine, and Nursing, the Saginaw Valley State University School of Nursing, and Kirtland Community College collaborate with MSU's cooperative extension service and communities in rural Michigan to offer services and training.
- *In West Virginia*, the University of West Virginia System encompassing Marshall University in Huntington, West Virginia University in Morgantown, and the West Virginia School of Osteopathic Medicine in Lewisburg partner with community health centers and local hospitals and their providers to meet rural health needs.

Independently, these academic community health systems, and the institutions and partners that shape them, are covering uncharted territory in health professions education, collaborative problem solving, and community-based learning and research. Collectively, the Community Partnerships stand to accomplish even more. By creating alternative models for health professions education to link with communities—and sharing the lessons learned along the way—the Community Partnerships with Health Professions Education initiative explores one viable solution to the shortage of primary care practitioners.

In the following eight chapters, the distinct elements of each

Community Partnership—academic health centers, communities, new linking organizations, policy, funding patterns, multidisciplinary education, and evaluation—are examined in depth. Each chapter details lessons learned by the Partnerships collectively as they addressed these critical features, and it provides background and guidance for others breaking new ground in their institutions and communities. Our hope is that describing the "nuts and bolts" of change as experienced through the Community Partnerships will support readers in initiating and sustaining alternative approaches to health professions education elsewhere.

3

....

An Update on the Community Partnerships

Rebecca C. Henry

The Community Partnerships with Health Professions Education initiative is made up of seven partnerships—communities linked with health professions educational institutions to help direct the education of health professionals by creating community-based, nonhospital teaching centers that stress primary health care education and research from a multidisciplinary approach.

This initiative has selected seven diverse educational models to foster the preparation of health professionals more interested in— and suited for—the practice of primary health care in communities. Each project has created a governance structure that bridges educational institutions and the community to create an effective partnership for sharing policy-making authority. These models provide the beginning organizational structures for the redirection of health professions education.

The seven projects represent multidisciplinary models for the delivery of primary health care services to defined populations, either through the creation of new centers or through the adaptation of existing ones. Some of the projects are urban; others are rural; two address both urban and rural areas. Some are based in metropolitan areas, and others are in smaller cities.

In addition to the academic dimension that combines teaching, service, and research in the nonhospital environment, these seven institutions have developed strategies to achieve a redirection toward sustained attention to primary health care education.

Georgia

Morehouse School of Medicine, in collaboration with Georgia State University's School of Nursing and Clark Atlanta University's programs in social work and allied health, has established partnerships with five federally funded community health centers and clinics. Together with community representatives, these institutions have established the nonprofit Southeastern Primary Care Consortium (SPCC), which serves as the organizational body responsible for the program. The SPCC board is made up of seven representatives from the health centers and related organizations, nine (including the board chairperson) from the communities served, eight from Morehouse School of Medicine, three from Georgia State University, and two from Clark Atlanta.

The five community health centers (some of which are multisite centers) constitute a comprehensive, multidisciplinary, academic primary care system. Interdisciplinary student teams (medical, nursing, social work, and allied health) are taught by comparably interdisciplinary faculty teams. These centers are gradually assuming a more academic character by expanding their educational and research activities.

New faculty with appropriate teaching, research, and patient care responsibilities have been added, and social work faculty and students play important roles. Community members and students from medicine, nursing, and social work link with neighborhood councils to facilitate the identification of needs and develop ways to approach those needs. Health education and outreach programs have been expanded, and connections with public schools have been strengthened.

The three educational institutions involved have collaboratively created new multidisciplinary educational experiences that are conducted in community settings: an introduction to primary care, a primary care practicum, and an introduction to community health. The medical school departments of community health/preventive medicine and family practice, the nurse practitioner programs, the social work program, and some allied health programs are all involved in all components of the practicum. The departments of pediatrics, obstetrics and gynecology, and medicine are also involved.

For all medical students, this represents 28 percent of the total curriculum. Within the medical school, the third-year activities have been completely revised, and all clinical specialties are collaborating on coursework that cuts across specialties and is delivered out-of-hospital. Georgia State University graduate nursing students spend 25 percent of their program in the multidisciplinary community settings. Approximately 30 percent of Clark Atlanta's social work students spend 20 percent of their curriculum time in the multidisciplinary experience.

Hawaii

The University of Hawaii has developed a partnership between its Schools of Medicine, Nursing, Social Work, and Public Health and five community health centers: the Waianae Coast Comprehensive Health Center, the Kalihi-Palama Health Clinic, the Queen Emma Clinic, the Kakua Kalihi Valley Community Health Center, and the Rural Oahu Health Center. The university's approach to developing model, comprehensive, multidisciplinary care systems for teaching, service, and research is to strengthen existing clinics.

The communities and patients served by each of the collaborating centers are very different and pose unique challenges in building community-based centers. In each case, community advocates are a basic element of the system. Services are provided at one high school, two elementary schools, and a housing project, in addition to clinic sites.

A nonprofit corporation, Ke Ola O Hawai'i, Inc., has been established to formalize the association between the University of Hawaii and the community health centers and to ensure community representation. A fourteen-member board guides the program. Board members include deans of the four health professions schools, a board member and administrative officer from each of the clinics, a provost from a community college, a state deputy director of health, and a representative from the physician community.

The School of Medicine has converted from a traditional, lecture-oriented curriculum to a problem-based, small-group approach. The School of Nursing has introduced inquiry-based classes, and all courses have become community-focused. This new format of small-group tutorials and self-directed learning lends itself especially well to decentralized sites for multidisciplinary instruction.

In the Kalihi-Palama neighborhood, students from the health professions schools serve as mentors to high school students in a new project called the Farrington High Health Academy. The project is designed to recruit and prepare students from this disadvantaged community to work in health fields.

Graduate-level nursing students spend twelve weeks for four semesters in the academic primary care centers. Social work undergraduate and graduate students and public health students spend between four and twenty-four hours per week in those centers throughout their programs. The community health centers are the primary educational site for 25 percent of medical school students.

Massachusetts

The Center for Community Health Education, Research, and Service (CCHERS) represents Boston and Northeastern Universities, city government, communities, and ten community health centers. CCHERS has developed a comprehensive model of care, education, and research; it has reformed curricula in nursing and medicine toward community-based learning; it has empowered residents living in identified communities to address their own needs; and it has developed leadership among partners. A twenty-two-member board representing all of the partners governs CCHERS and determines policy for its overall efforts. Majority control rests with community representatives.

Approximately 20 percent of Boston University School of Medicine's four-year curriculum is devoted to an integrated, continuous experience in the community health centers and communities. Students complete a community-based experience in their first year and are then assigned to the same community for the remaining three years of their work. Seven weeks in the third year and at least four weeks in the fourth are spent in the community health centers. For students in Northeastern's nursing program, approximately 50 percent of the total five-year curriculum is part of the new initiative. Students are introduced to community concepts in the first year of coursework. In subsequent years, students engage in community-based clinical experience with a particular community. Many of these nursing education experiences are multidisciplinary, involving medical students.

Each of the ten centers has shifted its activities to a multidisciplinary system—expanded to emphasize community, outreach, prevention, continuity, and coordination. Students work in teams to help neighborhoods identify needs and strengthen the centers' response to those needs. Selected physicians and nurses now on the staff are salaried for teaching purposes.

Community residents are actively involved in expanding outreach services and providing education. The Boston setting represents obvious social and economic problems that plague large inner cities.

Michigan

Community/University Health Partnerships (C/UHP) is a cooperative effort in interdisciplinary health professions education between Michigan State University's (MSU) Colleges of Human Medicine, Nursing, and Osteopathic Medicine and Saginaw Valley State University's (SVSU) College of Nursing and Allied Health Sciences. In the underserved rural northern Michigan communities of Alcona, Atlanta, East Jordan, Hillman, Houghton Lake, and Roscommon, and in the urban environments of Muskegon and Saginaw, community health centers have been adapted to educate medical and nursing students in a collaborative environment that stresses primary, rather than specialty, care.

An executive board oversees C/UHP functioning; but in the northern Michigan communities and the Saginaw area, separate not-for-profit organizations have also been formed to establish and foster the growth of health professions education in their regions. In Muskegon, the Muskegon Foundation has established a new subgroup—the Health Professions Education Council—to direct C/UHP activities in that region. The organizations directing local activities have representation from attorneys, bankers, health care professionals (doctors, nurses, pharmacists, hospital administrators, social workers, and so on), college presidents, retirees, and other community members. The involvement of community members in decisions about matters such as resource allocation, curriculum, and research has been beneficial in program development and implementation.

Each region has developed a strategic plan for ensuring that the models established by C/UHP will be sustained after the grant period has expired. In addition to the efforts of the governing bodies within each region, C/UHP has established the State Health Policy Council—made up of representatives of government, business, education, and C/UHP communities—to address policy issues relevant to C/UHP programs.

During the academic year 1993–94, more than seventy-five undergraduate and graduate nursing students from MSU and SVSU and over forty MSU medical students participated in the C/UHP curriculum. This curriculum, developed to be able to integrate concerns specific to each community, consists of multidisciplinary clinical experiences that take place at the various academic community health centers, weekly multidisciplinary didactic sessions, and regularly scheduled primary care seminars. Faculty from MSU and SVSU have been placed in communities to carry out both the clinical and didactic portions of the curriculum. In addition, primary care practitioners from the communities have been given appointments as clinical faculty. Where necessary, nurse practitioners have been hired to round out multidisciplinary faculty.

Tennessee

The Community Partnership in Tennessee links the Office of Rural and Community Health—part of East Tennessee State University's (ETSU) Division of Health Sciences—and ETSU's Schools of Nursing, Medicine, and Public and Allied Health. Through this partnership, ETSU has developed academic community health systems in two rural communities located one hour from its Johnson City campus. A wide variety of health and human service organizations have coalesced in developing community-based interdisciplinary educational experiences in schools, rural hospitals, mental health centers, private physician offices, industries, home health agencies, and nursing homes. A community-dominated governing board draws representation from community advisory boards and the deans of the three ETSU Health Sciences Colleges.

Students from nursing, medicine, and allied and public health form interdisciplinary cohorts. They commit to a regular schedule of community-based curricula that draws on the expertise of full-time community-based faculty and is linked with experiences throughout the academic community health system. Students also have clinical experiences in university-managed practices serving rural and underserved counties. The curriculum revolves around four themes: responsiveness to rural and community health needs, clinical skills development, interdisciplinary case conferences and collaboration, and community-based projects. Thirteen multidisciplinary courses have been developed, and these are required for students in all disciplines.

Additional rural curricular elements strengthen and build upon the interdisciplinary student efforts. The College of Nursing involves nursing students from the cohorts in a full-time community-based curriculum in Mountain City or Rogersville. Students live in these communities and take the vast majority of their courses using educational resources developed in the rural areas. The College of Medicine has developed an integrated four-month rural clerkship for students in their third year and a two-month experience for fourth-year students. It offers a combined educational experience to address clinical objectives in family medicine, internal medicine, pediatrics, psychiatry, obstetrics/gynecology, and surgery.

Texas

The University of Texas at El Paso (UTEP), Texas Tech University's Health Sciences Center in El Paso, and the Lower Valley Task Force (made up of health care consumers and providers in El Paso's Lower Valley) established the El Paso Institute for Community Health. This program has created school-based academic primary health clinics in the school districts of Fabens, San Elizario, Socorro, and Montana Vista. The Institute's objectives are to provide opportunities for health professions education, encourage health professions careers, develop a community-focused approach to health care, promote and coordinate community-based health research, encourage interdisciplinary collaboration, and develop a model program for linking community health workers with community people.

The Institute has a twenty-three-member advisory committee made up of the county judge and representatives from UTEP, Texas Tech, the Lower Valley Task Force, the city/county health department, the Lower Valley citizen committee, and the school districts. The Institute also works closely with the Area Health Education

Center (AHEC). The county constructed a school-based community health center in Fabens, and a fourth of the space it provides is earmarked for related academic programs. Medical and nursing teams work from a multisite system that includes the new county center and schools in the four districts serving the Lower Valley.

Thirty percent of the Texas Tech medical curriculum is based on the new school-based community health systems. All of the El Paso–based Texas Tech medical students have expanded opportunities for community-based educational experiences. Thirty percent of the students in each class participate in a community-focused curriculum that emphasizes multidisciplinary, nonhospital primary health care. A program for early identification and admission of Hispanic students has been undertaken to facilitate early selection of minority students, including qualified seniors at UTEP.

Twenty-six percent of undergraduate and 30 percent of graduate nursing students participate in a community-focused curriculum at UTEP. Significant portions of that curriculum reflect the community-based approach. El Paso Community College is also involved in meeting the dental needs of Socorro through the Institute. The community is having a dramatic impact on the academic institutions involved in the program.

West Virginia

The University of West Virginia System's (UWVS) seven health professions education programs—located at Marshall University of Huntington, West Virginia University Health Sciences Center in Morgantown, and the West Virginia School of Osteopathic Medicine in Lewisburg—are in widely divergent parts of the state. These institutions have collaborated with rural communities to transform primary care centers into rural academic centers for education, research, and service. They include three schools of medicine, two schools of nursing, a school of dentistry, and a school of pharmacy.

The University of West Virginia System has developed a multidisciplinary model of education and care that places faculty and students in rural primary care centers for a rotation of up to three months. Multidisciplinary student/faculty teams and community members collaborate in the development of multidisciplinary case studies; through these, students examine a wide range of problems and the impact of those problems on family health. Socioeconomic factors that influence the health and illness of individuals and families are integrated into these case studies. During discussions, campus-based faculty members and the field faculty interact with students from various disciplines, and community members participate as well. As of 1995, all health professions students in the state university system complete a rural rotation.

A joint governing committee made up of twelve community members and seven deans—a policy-making body—oversees the project. Community members represent minority groups (including women), business, industry, and labor.

The Kellogg Community Partnership Project has served as a model to make health professions education more responsive to the needs of rural communities throughout West Virginia. After the project was funded in 1991, the state's political leaders supported legislation that provided $6 million per year for the duration of the Kellogg project for the purpose of expanding the program to include other rural communities. This additional funding led to the development of the Rural Health Initiative. In 1995, legislation was approved that integrated the Kellogg projects and the Rural Health Initiative.

Summary of the Partnerships' Third-Year Progress Reports

Over time, the Community Partnerships are expected to produce more suitably prepared primary care practitioners to serve in communities of need than traditional health professions education produces. While a monitoring system is being implemented as the initiative progresses to track career choice and practice location, it is too early to collect data on graduates of the new program. However, an examination of other critical markers reveals a wealth of information on the progress of the Partnership concept. In the discussion that follows, these markers are described in terms of their relative importance, and data from the end of the third year are reviewed.

Organizational Structures

Each Community Partnership has created a governance structure of both community and educational institutional representatives to facilitate shared policy making. One indicator of joint decision making is the extent to which the community has a visible role in the overall organization. In the course of the initiative, Partnership boards have undergone a dramatic transformation. Initially, there was a powerful academic voice; currently, the boards have a much stronger community influence. In the first year of the Partnerships, only one board out of seven had a community majority; in the second year, that number grew to four, and now it is up to six. This steady trend signifies an extraordinary finding: academic institutions are capable of opening their traditional domains to include the community in shaping a more relevant curriculum for health professions students.

Both communities and academic institutions have experienced the risks and benefits of this nontraditional arrangement. The risks involve giving up some autonomy and power, but they are often offset by expansion of the political base for adopting important initiatives that support communities and health professions schools.

New Partners

Another important outcome, unintended at the start of the initiative, is an increase in the number of partners in each Community Partnership. In the first year, thirteen community-based academic health centers and twenty-four degree-granting health professions programs made up the Partnerships. By the end of the third year, that number had grown to thirty-eight academic health centers and twenty-nine degree-granting programs. The number of academic health centers is an important gauge that reveals the capacity of the Partnerships to educate and train students in out-of-hospital settings. Program watchers speculate that this increase may be one of the best measures of long-term sustainability. For most institutions, the extensive resources and effort involved in developing an academic health center forge a difficult commitment to break.

Curriculum Change

Educational reform takes place in a variety of different forms and with a range of impact. Unfortunately, much publicized "reform" never really changes institutions or the people who function within them. To determine whether the changes fostered by the Community Partnerships have impacted institutions and people, evaluators are monitoring the extent to which the Community Partnerships initiative produces permanent changes for the participating institutions. The changes required by Community Partnerships (and assessed by the evaluators) involve much more than simply finding new nonhospital settings for students. The Community Partnerships endeavor involves developing new or redesigning existing courses to support the new curriculum, presenting them for review to curriculum communities, reallocating budgets for the courses, and assigning appropriate faculty.

The list below reflects the extent to which new and significantly revised courses have emerged in the curricula of the academic institutions:

Total No. of New/ Revised Courses	Courses Offered in the Community	Required Courses	Courses Taught by Multi-disciplinary Faculty	Courses Taken by Multi-disciplinary Students
183	91	153	151	97

Course development has required substantial resources and faculty commitment in the first three years. Most notably, when the seven sites reported on course development in year one, there were no courses involving multidisciplinary faculty or students. Contrast that with the current statistics: 151 courses taught by faculty who are multidisciplinary and 97 courses taken by students from more than one health professions school. Because the vast majority of courses are required (and are approved by the curriculum committee), it is unlikely that these schools will return easily to their old curricula.

Institutional Policy Change

Policy changes made by the health professions schools are important indicators that these institutions are preparing to engage in permanent change. Institutional policies address the most important missions and functions of a school and ultimately define its purpose. To describe the character of the policy change, the efforts at change have been divided into four broad categories—those related to admissions and students, those related to curriculum, those related to faculty roles and responsibilities, and those related to multidisciplinary efforts—as shown in the following list:

Admissions and Students	Curriculum	Faculty Roles	Multi- disciplinary	TOTAL
14	52	19	10	95

New admissions policies might, for example, include appointing community health center faculty to the admissions committee or giving priority to an eligible student who resides in one of the targeted communities. Curriculum policies are frequently aimed at modifying required core coursework to include experiences in community centers. Faculty policies challenge old notions of what efforts and products may be used to build a faculty portfolio for tenure and promotion. (Scholarship conducted in communities may look different from university-based scholarship.) Finally, multidisciplinary policies are most likely to address ways in which different academic institutions can cooperate on shared course offerings, faculty appointments, and service delivery.

Faculty Involvement

Another marker of the progress the Partnerships have made in their first three years comes from the faculty themselves. The latest tally indicates that at least 527 faculty members from the participating health schools are actively involved in developing, teaching, and administering the new curricula. During uncertain financial times for universities, this demonstrates an extraordinary commitment to the Community Partnerships initiative. The vast majority of these faculty members volunteer their time on top of ongoing professional responsibilities.

The communities are also providing a generous number of teachers for this new initiative. To date, 778 professionals from the communities serve as teachers and mentors to our students. They play a critical role, assisting the students in understanding the importance of the community context in providing appropriate health care.

The following list shows the number of faculty members—teachers from the community as well as from academic institutions—at the Community Partnership academic institutions and health centers.

Academic Institutions	Total No. of Faculty
Atlanta	82
Hawaii	91
El Paso	16
MSU	46
ETSU	32
W. Virginia	220
Boston	40
TOTAL	527

Community Health Centers	Total No. of Faculty
Atlanta	205
MSU	154
Hawaii	23
ETSU	19
El Paso	16
W. Virginia	35
Boston	326
TOTAL	778

In monitoring faculty involvement in the initiative from the beginning, we have seen the number of faculty involved increase steadily. The second-year progress reports indicated that 1,182 faculty were involved in the initiative. In academic year 1993–94—the third year—that number exceeded 1,300. Furthermore, the progress reports reveal that the most rapid increase in faculty occurred in the community and not on campus at the institutions.

Contributed Dollars

Despite the significant funding provided by the Kellogg Foundation to support the development of these new community-based academic health centers, the financial contribution was not sufficient to implement the new model and prepare faculty and staff for their new roles. To date, the Partnerships themselves have combined to contribute more than $55 million to enhance the long-term viability of the models. This figure represents reallocated dollars from the health professions schools, in-kind contributions from the communities and schools, and grants from the communities and states. Table 3.1 presents the total number of contributed dollars by source.

Student Participation

This last critical marker represents the extent to which eligible students have begun to take courses in the new curriculum and have

Table 3.1. Resources Contributed to Partnerships by Academic
Institutions and Communities.

	Level of Institutional Support		
New	Reallocated	In-Kind	Subtotal
5,325,953	1,383,918	20,786,848	27,496,719
	Level of Community Support		
New	Reallocated	In-Kind	Subtotal
8,629,844	1,863,550	17,463,109	27,956,503
	Total Support		
13,955,797	3,247,468	38,249,957	55,453,222

been assigned to an academic community-based health system. The term *eligible* in this case reflects the actual number of students available to participate in Partnership activities, given an institution's requirements and schedule. Some institutions, for example, may have a program structure that makes it undesirable in a particular year for students to be off-campus in a community setting. Measuring participation against the number of eligible students thus presents a more meaningful denominator for comparison.

Table 3.2 describes participation levels across the different health professions programs. Most significant is the 20 percent of time the average Partnership student spends in a community setting. Certainly, the seven sites can testify that moving students out of hospitals and into community settings for such a substantial amount of time is no small effort.

Over the three-year period of this evaluation, the Community Partnerships have exhibited substantial gains in the number of students participating in the initiative, the number of centers and other out-of-hospital sites for student learning, the amount of student time dedicated to community learning, faculty participation, community participation, shared decision making, curricular and policy change, and financial commitment. While it is too early to declare the Community Partnerships a success, extraordinary progress has been made in these key areas.

Table 3.2. Summary of Student Participation.

Type of Student (all sites)	Students Involved		Time in Formal Classroom (% of total)	Time in Community (% of total)	Total % Time Initiative
	no. eligible	no. participating (and % of total)			
Medicine (ave. %)	2,492	1,228 (49%)	9%	17%	26%
Undergraduate Nursing (ave. %)	1,970	1,204 (61%)	21%	22%	43%
Graduate Nursing (ave. %)	663	416 (63%)	17%	25%	42%
Other (ave. %)	784	412 (53%)	9%	15%	24%
	5,909	3,260 (55%)	15%	20%	35%

4

How Public Policy Is Shaped

Ronald W. Richards

The politics of health care in the United States is chaotic. The politics of welfare reform is chaotic—as has been the politics of Social Security, national defense, civil rights, the war on poverty, and the North American Free Trade Agreement. Politics in this country is simply perpetually chaotic. That, many would say, was the intent of the founding fathers—a group of revolutionaries who had good reason to fear the arbitrary exercise of governmental power over people. The political system they designed is one that limits the easy acquisition of power by government and keeps policy in a continual state of flux.

There is no point, then, in waiting for the political climate to be *less* chaotic before tackling health professions educational reform. It will never be so. The inclinations of university-based leaders may be to defer action until some future time—a time when health policy is more settled. But if reform in health professions education is to succeed, those who lead it must consider the role of public policy in the change process from the very beginning—better yet, even before the beginning. Although the nature of academic health centers, the dynamics of community, and the development of structures for linking the two are all critical elements in reshaping the way health professionals are educated, no lasting change will occur unless the politics of making public policy is attended to from the start.

The differing cultures of community and academe play out in the policy arena as they do elsewhere. Yet achieving sustainable change in health professions education—change that is consistent with the interests of both cultures—requires change in public policies that tend to support the status quo.

Certainly, academics have done very well over the years at obtaining funds without paying much attention to what policy makers think. Seeking policy change is not generally considered the business of academe. The scholar's approach would likely be to wait until a model had proven itself, in a research sense, before supporting a related policy change. And academic institutions, like all organizations, are interested in preserving the status quo. As Victor Baldridge has remarked, universities and funds are like sponges and water: the one seems to be able to absorb great quantities of the other without any noticeable change in its character or structure.

Communities tend not to engage in the politics of policy making at all—at least where health professions education is concerned. In this arena, the community view appears to be that "experts know best." Local and state legislators, it would seem, agree. When a new notion about the education of health professionals surfaces, policy makers turn to their favorite academic experts for an opinion. Policy making, then, becomes circular: new ideas are promoted or discarded based on the opinion of those who have the most to lose from change. Not surprisingly, inaction is often the result.

Politics, at its core, is about the allocation of resources. Politics determines fundamentally who gets what according to what rules. In terms of health professions education, public policy is important because it influences both the allocation of resources and the allocation of decision-making authority over health care practice. The shift in focus from hospital-based to community-based education suggested by the Community Partnerships will be lasting only when the allocation of both funds and authority for health professions education is consistent with those educational reforms.

Public policy can be action-based or purposely inactive. In the

United States, public policy can be directive, as it often has been since the New Deal—calling upon government to set rules and fund projects accordingly—or it (and government) can do little or nothing, by the conscious choice of policy makers. In the case of health care policy in recent years, policy makers have chosen to do very little. As a consequence, market forces are establishing the rules.

Willie Sutton's oft-quoted retort—"That's where the money is"—offered when he was asked why he robbed banks, perhaps best explains the status of health professions education today. In the current policy climate, academic health centers receive public funds from local, state, and federal governments and private funds from insurance companies, HMOs, and businesses. The dollars they receive support patient care, research, and the education of the next generation of health professionals. Elaborate rules are set up to determine who gets these funds and under what conditions. Over the years, a status quo has emerged that promotes certain kinds of expenditures of public funds for these institutions. But now there are major challenges to this status quo. Some people suggest that all health care providers—instead of Medicare alone—should directly support the graduate education of health professionals. HMOs and other providers, these voices claim, should pay their share of graduate medical education—especially if they expect (as they should) to influence the curriculum of health professions education.

The present rules that govern expenditures are consistent with the economic interests of academic health centers and the continued production of medical specialists. In the two decades from 1971 to 1991, medical school earnings from clinical services grew from 12 percent of total revenues to 46 percent (Reinhardt, 1994). During a seven-year segment of that same time period (1982–1989), specialty preferences of medical school graduates showed an increase of 19 percent for psychiatry, 35 percent for anesthesia, 145 percent for dermatology, and 260 percent for physical medicine and rehabilitation (Garg, Boex, Davis, and Rodos, 1993). The type of education and services that academic health centers deliver nets considerable income under existing policies. Given these conditions, it is not surprising that most medical education is geared toward the hospital-based training of medical specialists. (In fact, such economic considerations are so critical that Chapter Eight addresses them in greater detail.)

The Community Partnerships with Health Professions Education initiative calls for a greater proportion of the education of health professionals to take place in communities than in tertiary care hospitals. However promising the initiative's Partnership models appear—and however much they accomplish for the communities they serve—no significant change will be sustained without a reallocation of funding to support the reforms they initiate and explore. Reform of health professions education is, then, a political process.

The Process of Making Policy

Much has been written about health policy and the policy-making process, especially since the federal health reform efforts of 1993 and 1994. The policy process is completed in four steps: (1) an issue is identified, (2) the issue is shaped, (3) solutions are proposed, and (4) legislative action is (or is not) taken. By law, neither a private foundation nor its grantees can expend funds on the fourth step in the process. It is appropriate, however, for foundations and their grantees to actively engage in the process of informing policy makers about issues, refining issues, and identifying possible solutions. For the Community Partnerships, then, it has been a matter of first deciding *whether* and then *how* to be involved in the initial three steps.

Public policy in our country is dominated by interest groups. Diverse groups advocate for policies favorable to their interests, and they do it with amazing vigor. Drug companies lobby for FDA and patent regulations to keep their businesses profitable; farmers advocate for wheat and corn price supports to do the same. In the area of health policy, trade associations (medical, nursing, and other), insurance companies, hospitals, durable medical equipment suppliers, and medical and nursing schools all exert considerable influence over the development of public policy related to health professions training and service delivery. At both the state and national levels, issues are driven by special interests and, increasingly, by the tide of public opinion (Knott, 1994).

Interest groups—whether they represent business, industry, trade or professional associations, or groups of consumers—seek to generate public interest and shape public opinion to create a sense of urgency related to their positions. When the public becomes concerned about an issue—the environment, taxes, the cost of health care—policy issues tend to emerge. The public's awareness and level of concern about a health or safety issue can also drive policy decisions. Public outcry about the use of the chemical Alar on apples is a perfect example of this dynamic.

Prior to 1989, the Natural Resources Defense Council, a nonprofit environmental advocacy group, had tried in vain to have Alar eliminated as a treatment for foodstuffs. Only with the well-orchestrated release of a study—and the overwhelming public response that followed—was the group able to accomplish its goal. Thanks to the media's extensive coverage, public awareness of the "health risk" surged. Response to the "danger" was immediate—people stopped eating apples—and in a very short time Alar was banned by federal regulation (Crossen, 1994).

While the real risk of Alar as a carcinogenic substance remains questionable, policy moved swiftly when public opinion rallied. In this case, an interest group used specific data to communicate with the public through media and evoke a policy response. Although the interrelation of data (evaluation and research), communication, and policy are seldom so vividly portrayed, public policy is often the result of these three factors.

Health workforce policy—the policy arena that most closely impacts health professions education—is not generally an area of public concern. Although public anxiety about the cost of health care and coverage for the uninsured has ebbed and flowed in recent years, people do not readily see a connection between the policy that governs allocation of public dollars for health professions training and their health care worries. Market, state, and federal attempts to "fix" health care, most people would say, are complex and confusing enough.

Even in the absence of comprehensive reform, new governmental rules are being fashioned to control costs. Federal, state, and local budgets are being cut. Health insurance companies and HMOs are trying to increase revenues and reduce costs. In this chaotic context, health professions educational reform seems a minor point. But to effect reforms in the long run, those seeking change in communities and institutions must inform public opinion and policy makers at the local, state, and federal levels about the relevance of health professions education to the availability, quality, and cost of health care.

The shaping of policy begins locally and moves back and forth through various democratic processes to effect change at state and federal levels. Built into the U.S. character—and thus its systems—are an independent nature, a positive attitude toward the private sector, and a distrust of government intervention. Domestic policy solutions tend to flow not *from* Washington but *to* it. Congress, in the process of representing voters and interest groups, seeks compromise and acts to modify proposed programs based on the preferences of these groups. State legislators, no less advocates for their constituents, do the same. Thus policy solutions are not generated by policy makers in most cases; they come from outside government.

Reforming health professions education requires that institutions and communities plunge into the chaos of the real world, seeking to understand the nuances of the policy-making process and the national and state policy implications of their local efforts. The decision to become involved in informing policy is not a simple one for Community Partnerships projects. All Partnership participants—whether from academe or the community—have their own interests. Each of them, in fact, probably represents other organizations that directly or indirectly engage in the policy process. Across all of the Partnerships, the question of whether to be involved in the public policy process tests the existence of a transcending vision and an overriding purpose for the Partnership organization.

Some Community Partnerships have engaged in the process of informing policy. Of these, some have taken positions on prescription privileges for nurse practitioners, the allocation of state funds for school-based clinics, and the most appropriate allocation or reallocation of funds for the sustainability of the Partnership itself. Other Community Partnerships have not been involved in the policy process, choosing instead to maintain allegiance to the organizations represented around the Partnership table. Those representing academe, for example, might support an unrestricted increase in operating funds for universities and community colleges. For representatives of community organizations, the highest priority might be an increased Medicaid appropriation for prenatal care.

Whatever the decision with regard to informing policy, both the nature and the extent of a project's involvement need to be determined. In one way or another, the Community Partnerships and the Kellogg Foundation return to three pivotal questions: How can a Community Partnership contribute to issue identification? How can a project participate in shaping that issue? How can the lessons learned through model development best be communicated to policy makers? In response to these questions, the Community Partnerships initiative has fostered federal, state, and local activity.

Issue Identification

With regard to health care delivery systems, the Kellogg Foundation identified its issues long ago: more and better community-based primary care and public health care will make health care more affordable and accessible to people at a cost society can afford. Since the 1930s, the Foundation has called attention to these issues, helped to shape these issues, and funded models from which lessons might be learned. And beginning in 1991, with the Community Partnerships with Health Professions Education initiative, the Kellogg Foundation targeted the issue of more suitably prepared primary care practitioners working together in nonhospital settings.

In a neutral fashion—free from the biases of political parties and interest groups—the Kellogg Foundation seeks to help projects individually and collectively educate policy makers. Consumers, payers, providers, educators, and policy makers have been identified as key audiences, and common messages ("More primary care practitioners are needed"; "Current funding supports the production of medical specialists in hospitals") have been developed to support the concept of out-of-hospital, multidisciplinary health professions education.

The Kellogg approach in this initiative is based on five observations:

1. While not much was expected from the federal discussion of the early 1990s, something labeled health care reform would result.

2. Health workforce policy would not be a heavily debated public issue, but it would be seen as a bipartisan one, and changes would be attached to a reform bill.

3. It would require considerable education of policy makers to bring about funding for out-of-hospital education.

4. Whatever the conclusion of the congressional debate, federal policy could not be ignored, because the majority of public funding for health professions education—more specifically, graduate medical education—was coming from federal sources.

5. The attention on health reform would positively affect the sustainability of the Community Partnerships projects.

Issue identification on the part of the Community Partnerships has been characterized by several features: the important issues were decided very early; efforts of the Community Partnerships to inform policy have been both concrete and abstract; the strategy has been multipronged, to include evaluation, communication, and the projects.

Issue Shaping

Educational reforms such as those suggested by the Community Partnerships are local models that can serve to inform and strengthen public policy at the community, state, and federal levels:

- Locally, the work of the Community Partnerships has policy implications for academic institutions, hospitals, insurance companies, business coalitions, and health providers. Policies may impact reimbursement for services delivered locally, allocation of resources to institutions, and regulation of health professions and service sites.

- In the state and federal arenas, existing policies govern appropriations (to academic health centers and teaching hospitals), reimbursement (for services delivered), regulation (of nurse practitioners, physician assistants, and so on), subsidies (to medical schools for primary care programs), and incentives (tax breaks and loan forgiveness).

Those seeking to reshape health professions education need to develop strategies related to policy at multiple levels to support and sustain change. The strategies need to recognize the role that data (evaluation and research) and communication play in successfully informing policy, and they must include evaluation and communication staff in planning and execution. To assist the Community Partnerships in this process, each Partnership developed an "integrated action plan"—an analysis of policy objectives along with a systematic approach to first identifying the information needs of policy makers and the public and then developing the appropriate communication tools to meet them.

While many of the policy goals that the Community Partnerships identified early in the process were geared toward changes in local and institutional policy (reallocation of university general funds, new faculty positions, faculty promotion and tenure, managed-care arrangements, and so on), promising strategies for sustaining the Partnerships beyond the grant period by informing state and federal policy have also emerged.

The Community Partnerships have identified a variety of policy modifications that would sustain and expand project activities beyond the granting period:

- Increase the state's unrestricted appropriation to institutional partners.

- Seek a specific state appropriation for each Partnership.

- Amend scholarship and loan policies to support primary care in underserved areas.

- Increase primary care program support.

- Increase state support of community health centers.

- Change the reimbursement rate for primary care providers.

- Modify regulations governing nurse practitioners.

- Garner support from payers for community-based education.

- Expand support for family practice residency programs.

- Offer incentives for racial and ethnic representation among health professions students.

- Redirect graduate medical education funding.

To take positive steps toward policy education, Community Partnerships have employed an assortment of strategies during the first three years of the initiative. Some of these strategies are highlighted below.

Developing a Position Paper or Report

At the end of the second year, four of the Community Partnerships gathered information about current policy, compared it to what was being learned through their community-based programs, and created a formal paper to share findings with policy makers, public officials, and their staff.

Seeking Support from Purchasers, Payers, and Providers

Several Community Partnerships have worked at the local and state levels to inform purchasers (business coalitions), payers (insurance companies, HMOs, and so on), and providers (medical societies and professional associations) of the opportunities and mutual benefits that community-based education of health professionals affords.

Engaging the Local Communities to Connect with Policy Makers

Some Community Partnerships, recognizing the strong linkages many community members have with elected officials, have worked through their community representatives to communicate with policy makers at the state level.

Providing Testimony at Legislative Hearings or Committees

A number of Community Partnerships have sought opportunities to offer testimony on related issues as a way of expanding legislators' awareness of and interest in the possible benefits of community-based health professions education.

Collaborating with Other Initiatives

Some Community Partnerships have integrated their efforts with other major initiatives to broaden their base of support, form productive linkages for Partnership efforts, and raise awareness of project goals and activities.

Meeting with Selected Policy Makers

Four Community Partnerships have met with influential elected officials at the state and federal levels to identify policy issues relative to Partnership objectives and to familiarize legislators with the Community Partnerships model. These Partnerships have also invited members of the legislative and executive branches of state government to tour Partnership sites and see firsthand what community-based health professions education can accomplish.

Establishing Alliances with Other Community-Based Policy Groups

Several Community Partnerships have linked up with groups sharing a mutual interest in expanding the role of the community in planning and decision making. Associations of this type help Partnerships recognize the policy implications of their efforts and create a base from which to inform the legislative process.

Working Through the University to Inform State Policy Decisions

Some of the Community Partnerships have addressed policy issues and their long-term implications through university discussions on primary care and other areas of concern affecting health professions training.

Developing a Communication Plan

Many of the Community Partnerships have developed detailed communication plans to ensure that approaches to informing the general public, business, providers, and policy makers are part of a systematic effort over a period of time.

Policy Lessons

Although jumping into the "real world" of policy is not easy for many of those interested in reforming the education of health professions, the benefits of taking the plunge are very real indeed. In the process of identifying policy issues and exploring ways of impacting them, the Community Partnerships have collectively happened upon a few pitfalls and ferreted out some useful approaches to addressing the role of public policy in sustaining change. Among their hard-learned lessons are these:

- *The policy process is not well understood.* In Washington, D.C., and the state houses, the four-step process described earlier is common knowledge. But among the leadership of academe and communities—those who can best guide health professions educational reform—the dynamics of informing policy are not readily understood. Learning how policy works and recognizing the legitimate function of informing policy options by sharing information about promising models are requirements for those who seek to lead educational reform.

- *All politics is local.* Tip O'Neill's (1994) famous comment says it best: even federal activity requires input—ideas, encouragement, practical models—from local projects. During the debate over federal health care reform in 1993 and 1994, one U.S. senator became a vocal supporter of change in workforce policy in part because of what he learned from the Community Partnership in his home state. Another U.S. senator learned of a Community Partnership's work from his constituency. Local work can and does serve to inform policy options over time and demonstrates models that hold promise for policy modification.

- *A common vision is critical to eveloping and addressing policy objectives.* The Community Partnerships bring together the competing interests of institutions and communities. In addressing policy issues, as in other critical areas of functioning, a clear collective vision is crucial to achieving impact. Communities may see the role of the Partnership in terms of providing needed services in the community. Health professions education faculty interested in reform may cast the problem as one of too few generalists rather than too many specialists—or too few adequately prepared primary care providers. Without a shared vision of Partnership goals, "partners" can differ greatly in how they define policy interests. Representatives of community organizations and academic institutions need to recognize their differences, openly address problems, be willing to put aside their separate interests, and craft policy objectives around common interests.

• *Policy interests must be shaped by community and academe together.* Communities tend to look to academic institutions to take the lead in setting and achieving policy objectives—despite the fact that they themselves are often closer to policy makers and issues. And representatives from academe—who have institutional constraints on their involvement with policy and a very different view of issues and needs—are often less than comfortable with the political process. If the seven Community Partnerships had not been required to address policy implications through the integrated action plan process, most would have avoided the politics of public policy altogether. But addressing policy is a legitimate role for those seeking to sustain change in health professions education. Despite the difficulties, conflicts, and varying comfort levels of dealing with politics, public policy has a significant impact on the long-term viability of educational change. By working together, community and academe are better able to carry the message to policy makers and the public. And, together, the message they carry has far more impact.

• *Leaders need to be aware of the positions of their national constituent organizations.* Health policy is of primary interest to numerous groups and professional associations, and every one of them takes a position on key issues. To understand the breadth of an issue and the range of influences affecting policy development, leaders of health professions educational reform need to be aware of these positions—especially those that reflect the opinion of peers in the academic, medical, or nursing communities. Medical school deans, for example, need to be aware of the Association of American Medical Colleges' position on policy issues. Nursing school deans need to keep current with the American Nurses Association positions. Among the health professions, physicians, nurses, public health workers, and others often take differing views on policy issues. To anticipate this type of fragmentation and better prepare for addressing divergent positions, those who would lead educational change must be well informed about the larger policy context and the positions of national constituent groups.

• *Evaluation and communication must have a prominent role in developing policy interests.* High-profile interest groups are very adept at the process of gathering relevant data and communicating it to policy makers, the business community, providers, and the general public. To successfully address public policy, projects such as the Community Partnerships must develop these skills as well. Projects must begin early to identify what key audiences need to understand and how best to communicate with them. Evaluators must strive to understand the policy process and learn what type of information is needed to adequately inform policy makers. As project activities unfold, evaluation must assume an "inside" role, providing grist for communication with groups that have a stake in the process. Both evaluation and communication functions must be closely linked with leadership in the process of identifying policy issues and objectives. By adapting these functions into a combined effort, projects of modest size can begin to impact the development of public policy relative to their goals.

• *Timing is everything.* In several states, the policy context is changing at a breakneck pace. The states of Hawaii and Tennessee have overhauled their entire reimbursement and delivery systems, for example, and before long they may overhaul them again. Other states have made less dramatic, but no less sweeping, health policy changes. Still others are contemplating them. This dynamic environment is fraught with opportunities for those with strong links to policy makers and viable options to demonstrate. Although the natural instinct of many is to wait and see what develops at the state and federal levels, those who wade into the choppy waters of these uncertain times may be well rewarded for their efforts. Whatever the solutions to the crises in the national and state health care systems, more primary care professionals will be an absolute necessity. There is a place for workforce policy modification in every reform effort.

• *Understanding the nature and importance of policy activity takes time and effort.* Although in the abstract the link between public policy and local reform efforts may be understandable, the complexity of policy issues and the myriad forces at work in policy contexts make these issues very difficult to grasp. Armed with the best of intentions and with tangible incentives for acting, most Partnership leaders have found moving in policy circles a daunting experience. As part of the Community Partnerships initiative, the Kellogg Foundation has supported some broad-based information gathering and provided a number of opportunities for networking and dissemination at the regional and national levels. But even with this entrée, most Partnerships have been slow to address policy issues. Anticipating this natural reticence, leaders of educational reform must put policy issues at the center of sustainability and keep them there to produce lasting change. Time, energy, and resources must be allocated to meet policy objectives from a project's inception.

In 1993 and 1994, the federal debate on health care heightened general awareness of public policy issues relative to health reform among the Community Partnerships and elsewhere. Yet for all the debate about health care reform, the need to reform the education of health professionals received very little attention. Some workforce issues were not debated: the fact that the federal government pays 50 percent of the total costs of the education of medical specialists to hospitals, the fact that the current system supports 100 percent of U.S. medical school graduates and an additional 40 percent of international medical students. And no legislation was passed, of course. The debate and inaction demonstrated again that revolution of any kind at the national level is not part of the U.S. form of democracy.

But the concerns that brought this issue to the forefront of national policy—the concerns of this country's citizens about access to health care, the cost of health care, and the possible loss of insurance coverage—are still with us, and the concerns are growing in number and importance. There is a mismatch between graduates' skills and experience and the jobs that await them in the health care industry. There is a mismatch between what people want from health care and how public money is being expended for health professions education. These mismatches will be addressed at some point through the policy process. For those who wish to take the lead in health professions education reform, the policy environment cannot be ignored.

5

The Nature of Academic Health Centers

Ronald W. Richards

Young people entering health professions education expect to be trained in hospitals as surely as they expect TV medical dramas to take place in frantic emergency rooms, pressure-filled hospital waiting rooms, and rambling urban medical centers. Doctors, nurses, and hospitals are inseparable in popular culture. And with good reason: academic health centers—university-affiliated tertiary care hospitals—are at present the primary site for medical and nursing education in the United States. Of the 141 medical schools in this country, most function as part of an academic health center that links health professions education—the training of medical, nursing, pharmacy, public health, and other students—with one or more teaching hospitals. Although the major centers among these make up only 4.2 percent of U.S. hospital facilities, they train 67 percent of all medical residents (Matherlee, 1994).

The Rise of Academic Health Centers

Hospital-based health professions education is the standard in our country and has been for almost a century. The notion of the academic medical center was modeled on the Johns Hopkins School of Medicine (founded in 1893) and spread by the findings of the Flexner Report in 1910. The "Johns Hopkins model," as Howard Brody (Brody and others, 1993) calls it, was developed in response to four pressing issues in the late 1880s. Brody notes that physicians were poorly trained in the biological sciences, this country had no "institutional base" for importing and building on the scientific strides being made in Europe, there was no appropriate setting in which well-trained physicians could apply their knowledge to patient care and student training, and there was no method of adapting rural medical practice and training to the needs of a growing industrialized society.

The Johns Hopkins model linked hospital-based training with scholarly research, patient care, and university classes in the physical sciences. Although a renegade approach to medical training in its time, the threefold mission of academic health centers—research, patient care, and teaching—gained credence in the first part of the twentieth century and produced measurable improvements in health outcomes after 1940 (Brody and others, 1993).

During the 1950s and early 1960s, an influx of federal research funds from the National Institutes of Health (NIH) financed significant expansion in these institutions. A belief in the potential of research to produce even more improved health outcomes fueled the steady flow of research dollars to medical school departments and teaching hospitals. Research grants financed much of the growth during this period and narrowed the educational perspective of academic health centers toward subspecialization. Individual departments receiving grants were able to add staff, attract promising students as research fellows, and support expanded laboratory and research facilities. As the scholarship of individual departments added stature and resources to an academic institution, the clinical interests of department leadership and faculty quite naturally began to shape the institution's curriculum and mission.

In 1965, the enactment of Medicare and Medicaid provided an additional source of revenue to the university teaching hospital. Billing for patient care services—delivered by and under the supervision of faculty—gradually supplanted research as a major contributor to the teaching hospital's budget (Garg, Boex, Davis, and

Rodos, 1993; Matherlee, 1994). In 1963–64, patient care revenues made up only 3 percent of U.S. medical school budgets, while federal funding—granted primarily for research—provided more than 54 percent of total revenues. In 1970–71, patient care services contributed 12 percent of medical school funding. By 1991–92, U.S. medical schools obtained more than 46 percent of revenues from delivering medical services (Reinhardt, 1994). In the twenty-five years from 1960 through 1985, while funding for research from the NIH increased sixfold, clinical revenues to academic health centers grew twentyfold (Cohen, 1994b).

With proceeds from both research and patient care services available, individual medical school departments continued to flourish throughout the 1970s and 1980s. Because qualifying for reimbursement as a graduate medical education (GME) program was not linked to any specific curricular content, the procedure-driven Medicare payment system supported expanded specialist training in teaching hospitals.

Then, in 1983, Congress amended the Social Security Act to create a prospective payment system. By establishing diagnosis-related groups (DRGs) to guide Medicare reimbursements, Congress changed the market forces affecting health care delivery in general and medical education specifically. Physicians at academic medical centers, accustomed to keeping patients in hospital beds for a few extra days to run tests and train students, could no longer count on reimbursement through GME payments for the hospital's additional costs. Leaders in medical education challenged the fairness of the new reimbursement structure. Under the new guidelines, they protested, academic health centers could not successfully compete in the marketplace. Because their purpose was to train students, the costs related to their facilities and services would always be higher. How could they attract patients to their facilities, they reasoned, if their costs were substantially higher? And without patients, how could they train medical students?

To reduce the "burden" to academic health centers imposed by the DRG system, Congress established a mechanism for GME indirect payments to be made to teaching institutions in addition to the direct payments for patient care. GME indirect payments subsidized academic health centers and in effect freed them from the constraints of market forces. With independent sources of funding for their interests and government subsidies to compensate for the demands of market forces, medical school departments and the academic health centers they link with have been able to pursue subspecialty research and health professions training with few limitations.

In the presence of such rich resources, the university teaching hospitals of the early twentieth century have evolved into the academic health centers that anchor health professions education in the United States today. At present, academic health centers are regarded as the premier sites for health professions education, research, and scholarship. These institutions are at the hub of the nation's health professions education, biomedical and health services research, and patient care services (Howe, Osterweis, and Rubin, 1994). Virtually all medical and nursing education takes place within classroom walls and academic health centers, and almost all public funding for health professions education is tied to the activities of these institutions.

Yet as academic health centers have risen in stature, the sphere of influences affecting them (and, by association, the medical schools they define) has narrowed considerably. In the course of their evolution, teaching hospitals—once largely philanthropic institutions bound to and by the needs of the community—have grown to depend on funding from the research and teaching that individual departments direct. And the thriving medical school departments, increasingly successful in obtaining research dollars and fees for patient care services, have grown less and less dependent on the academic institutions that fostered their development.

By endorsing the expansion and growth of academic health centers, teaching hospitals and universities have unwittingly weakened their own influence over this successful offspring and moved away from their original mission. As Brody observes, "The followers of Johns Hopkins, influenced by the money that flows from research grants and from high-technology patient care, often seem to have forgotten that they exist to teach" (Brody and others, 1993, p. 1098).

As with all of health care in the United States, however, the situation for academic health centers in the 1990s is changing dramatically. For years, academic health centers responded to and influenced the policies that shaped their funding. In 1963, the Health Professions Educational Assistance Act was passed by Congress. In 1971, the Comprehensive Health Manpower Training Act followed. Through federal legislation, the public demanded an increase in the number of health professionals, and academic health centers responded. The passage of Medicare and Medicaid also had a profound impact, of course, on academic health centers, health professions education, and health care. By one description, these programs "contributed to the decline of city-county hospitals as the prevailing site of medical education, changed the social contract between a patient and student physician, promoted the expansion of medical schools by unleashing a tidal wave of pent up demand, focused attention on the medical problems of minorities, the aged, and the disabled, altered the financing of faculty activity, and pushed faculties into a more direct role in patient care. By making all patients 'private' Medicare and Medicaid have eased the way for educational programs in truly private patient settings" (Wilson and others, 1983, p. 21).

Today academic health centers find themselves in the difficult predicament of trying to catch up to public policy and the demands of market forces. At the heart of the complexities facing academic health centers as they try to adapt is the tug-of-war between managed care and fee-for-service practice. What people want in their health system—more comprehensive primary health care—and what public policies are paying for place academic health centers

squarely in the middle of the fray. The revolution in human genet-
ics and the importance of recent discoveries to the long-term health
of the general public further complicate the landscape (Howe,
Osterweis, and Rubin, 1994). In all of this, the related costs to society underscore the need to strike some balance between the immediate benefits of primary care and the potential boons of research
and technology.

Academic health centers are in a state of flux, to be sure. Certain organizational characteristics they possess may constrain their
ability to respond to changing expectations, however.

Organizational Characteristics of Academic Health Centers

Academic health centers are made up of groups of distinct professions, each pursuing its professional work in relative independence.
In this respect, they are like universities in organization and structure. Universities are very different from corporate or governmental organizations—the IBMs and GMs of the world. They are
formed not by function or in relation to a central goal or product.
Universities are collections of individuals with very different types
of expertise linked together. They tend to foster differentiation
among their many parts. Although the tendency to differentiate—
to specialize and narrow a segment of knowledge or work to secure
a position of prominence—is common to all organizations, universities (like other professional organizations) are often *defined* by this
trait.

A university is a loosely organized, interrelated system of units,
each representing a discrete group of professionals. Each unit—
whether it be microbiology, Renaissance literature, or dance—is
defined by the content of its subject rather than by its place in the
larger organization. Individual departments in these structures are
driven not by the mission of the larger institution that houses them
but by the needs and interests of faculty members and the particular

segment of the profession they pursue. Universities are necessarily differentiated, since the subject and work of a unit or department cannot be completely known by those outside it. But because universities are served almost exclusively by professionals at the peak of their respective professions, the characteristics of these groups tend to dictate the larger organization's structure.

Andrew Abbott makes the point that "the essence of a profession is its work not its organization" (1988, p. 112). The content and control of that work, he explains, defines a profession and its members. And the ways in which members of a profession seek to delineate and expand their "work" are many. They capitalize on external changes, for example—position vacancies and other organizational events that create opportunity for expansion. Or they redefine their work to encompass a new, previously unrelated problem or issue by reducing the issue to the scope of their work. Abbott cites the example of the problem of child misbehavior. If misbehavior is "reduced" to hyperactivity, he says, it becomes a medical problem and part of a physician's "work" (p. 98). Professions are expert at this type of reduction—at defining problems in terms of their expertise—and in doing so, they enlarge the scope of their professional work.

The tendency toward internal differentiation to create new roles is another key characteristic of organizations dominated by professionals, whatever their profession (Bucher and Stelling, 1977). Rather than assuming an existing role in an organization, individual professionals tend to build new roles around their unique expertise. To accomplish such an expansion or shift, professionals engage in open negotiation with "relevant figures"—a department's power brokers and others who will be involved in the development of a new work interest or professional linkage. Rue Bucher and Joan Stelling identify use of time and space to support a professional interest as the determining factor in a faculty member's role definition. Faculty members seeking to carve a niche for themselves, they say, negotiate for laboratory space, resources, and professional time to secure the freedom to do their work, and thus they secure their place in the department.

Bucher and Stelling believe that organizations of professionals are integrated through a political process rather than social structure. Professionals seek to influence goal setting and policy within their organizations. They lobby openly for resources, acknowledging that they are in competition with other professionals for the time, money, and space they need to do their professional work. Differing values and conflicting interests support an ongoing political process of negotiation through a series of committees, senates, and faculty meetings (1977, p. 132). Participants in this process— faculty, department heads, and to some extent deans—form alliances around issues and extend quid pro quo support much as members of Congress do. Although the tone and scope of the debate is modest by comparison, the dominant mechanism of decision making in professional organizations is legislative in nature.

Bucher and Stelling observe that, within the dynamic political environment of organizations dominated by professionals, power is a fluid commodity. Influence is based on linkages and resources rather than position within the organization. A dean may hold her position for decades, but the position does not necessarily come with influence. Influence—or power—is traded in a different currency. A new faculty member may have a great deal of influence when he lands a sizable NIH grant; department heads and other faculty may seek his involvement and support on issues while the grant is in place. But relations between the department head and the new faculty member may fade if no new source of support emerges as the granting period wanes. The locus of power in this setting shifts easily. It comes and goes as different faculty and issues move through the department or university.

These tendencies—to differentiate among professions within a university or educational organization, to build new roles within the organization rather than assuming existing ones, to openly negotiate for autonomy and resources, to integrate within the organization through a political process, to recognize power based on resources and linkages rather than position—characterize academic health centers and medical schools in particular.

Health professions education schools and the academic health centers they work through are highly differentiated. To the outside world, a medical school, for example, may seem to represent a single entity. But to those functioning inside its walls, a medical school is a collection of departments linked only loosely to the larger organization. Each individual department has its own objectives related to its chosen field of study—its work. Departments of medicine may have a neurology section; but pediatric departments have pediatric neurology, and physiology departments have neurophysiology. Each department brings in revenue and resources independent of other departments in the school. Each department controls these resources and thus holds the power of reward over its members and their careers. In medical schools, faculty in departments with grants for research and with income from supervising patient care often hold more real power than most university deans.

Within medical school departments, a continuous process of definition and redefinition, alignment and realignment, is at work. If the assumption that a profession does better and better work if it focuses on smaller and smaller pieces of a problem is widely accepted, the opportunities to redefine professions within a profession are virtually unlimited. Frequently, pieces of this differentiated structure are reformed into some new organizational entity—the various neurology sections listed above, for instance, might group themselves into a department of neurosciences to achieve greater influence and acquire independent financial support. But the movements within these structures are seldom aimed at coordinating departments or consolidating into fewer departmental units. The departments that compose academic health centers tend rather to become more fragmented and decentralized, spawning new circles within circles as they more narrowly define the part of the whole that their members examine professionally.

While the influence of revenues and resources is paramount in academic health centers, nursing schools have adapted in fundamentally different ways to establish independence in this dynamic environment. They have tended to align themselves with university value systems and have worked more closely than academic health centers with people in communities (Grace, 1990). Where medical schools have exerted enormous control over their development by securing independent sources of income, nursing schools have traditionally worked through university channels to sustain their activities. Gender differences may account in part for these divergent approaches. Medicine, historically dominated by men, has worked through power structures and economic forces. Nursing, guided primarily by women, has sustained itself by building networks, expanding communication, and aligning its interests with the weak and powerless. In some views, nursing has taken an adversarial position in relation to medicine—focusing on keeping people in communities and out of hospitals. From this competitive stance, Helen Grace explains, nurses "surrender" patients to the medical care system only if they "fail."

Such differences among academic health center participants, little understood or acknowledged, support the pervasive differentiation among health professions schools and departments and further contribute to the separateness characteristic of these environments.

Manifestation of Differentiation in Academic Health Centers

Differentiated organizations such as these do not change or adapt to new ways readily. In fact, with no central mission or shared vision to guide them, they tend to resist change. These departmentalized, hierarchical organizations, lacking in strong, influential leadership, are generally less successful at implementing change than more centralized structures are (Kanter, 1984; Goodman and Dean, 1980, cited in Bland, Starnaman, Zonia, and Rosenberg, 1992). In four specific areas—curriculum, evaluation of students, approaches to student training, and faculty rewards—the tendency to differentiate has significant effects on academic health centers' ability to adapt to change.

Attempts to modify curriculum illustrate the complexities of initiating change in differentiated settings. In health professions schools, departments tend to administer the curriculum—course by course. Department faculty serving on committees represent their individual departments' interests. Questions of the "relative advantage" or "relevance" of curricular components are shaped by the perspectives and needs of those who will administer them. The values and procedures of a department and its faculty may differ greatly from the values and procedures of colleagues in the next department, and all are competing for student time and attention. The debate over what makes a good doctor, nurse, dentist, or pharmacist is inevitably shaded by the subtext of curriculum committee members to mean, What knowledge from our department must a competent graduate possess?

Curriculum adaptation in health professions schools is further hampered by the widespread use of behavioral objectives in curriculum development. Health professions schools produce sets of behavioral objectives by the thousands and turn them over to curriculum committees to make rational decisions about what knowledge is prerequisite for these behaviors. Rather than broadening the focus of what is taught, the use of behavioral objectives tends to narrow the focus to increasingly minuscule portions of the whole. The driving question behind this approach to curriculum is this: What specifically should be taught? More philosophical questions—Why is this important? Where and by whom can this best be taught?— are not often raised. And yet these latter questions hold the most promise for curriculum improvement and productive change in health professions education.

Just as differentiation among departments shapes curriculum development, it also dictates the mode of evaluation. In fact, student assessments are all too often the basis for the behavioral objectives that curriculum committees use to make decisions. The mastery of behavioral objectives is generally measured by comprehensive, multiple-choice examinations. Recall of facts tends to be the subject of student evaluation; application of knowledge to clinical decision making has only recently gained some ascendancy. The narrower the subject, the more specific the facts to be recalled (and, some claim, later discarded).

The view that education is a rational process rooted in the acquisition of fact-based knowledge undergirds this approach to evaluation. It implies that memorization is the key skill needed to produce a competent practitioner and that the mastery of ever smaller bits of information will best prepare the health professional for the rigors of the profession. Allocation of student time in this environment is the product of intense negotiation between individual departments of health professions schools on behalf of their uniquely defined profession. How much time the student is allowed to watch and learn from the primary care practitioner versus the subspecialist is dictated by the same influences that define and redefine curriculum within the health professions school. Individual parts of departments and schools compete for student time to ensure that soon-to-be graduates have adequate time to "see and do" the work of their particular segment of the profession. Lacking the chance to "show and tell" their work to students, generalists—usually working outside of hospitals—have little opportunity to define the profession in their terms.

Differentiation impacts the system of faculty rewards in academic health centers just as significantly. The more specialized a field of study, the less likely it is that others outside it will have the skill to evaluate the competency of its members. Under these circumstances, tenure committees have little chance of evaluating the skill of a faculty member specializing in an area outside their own expertise. And the more areas of expertise there are, the more common the problem. To manage this limitation, tenure committees have taken to allowing experts in a given field to endorse the competence of their faculty. They look to the individuals on the editorial boards of refereed journals, for example, or those who award NIH grants to tell them what they need to know. By selecting a faculty member's article for publication or providing funding for his or her research, recognized authorities affirm that individual's research competence. By counting the number of articles accepted for publication or measuring the funding awarded, a tenure committee can presumably determine the most able among its faculty.

This focus on "quality research productivity" is the most widely used measure of a faculty member's worth and has come to define scholarship in education. As Ernest Boyer states, "According to the dominant view, to be a scholar is to be a researcher" (1990, p. 2)—and the reward system in place reinforces this paradigm. But in some medical schools, not all faculty members do research. Many are clinical faculty who work in hospitals and generate income through patient care. The limitations of a highly differentiated academic department become all too clear when the issue of faculty rewards is raised. How can clinical faculty receive tenure and the rewards that accompany it in this system? Consistent with the nature of academic health centers—and the organizations of professionals in general—the predominant approach is to differentiate. Many health professions schools create a clinical tenure track—a new and separate part of the larger system with its own rules, faculty, and interests—to solve the problem.

Academic Health Centers and the Public Trust

Academic health centers—these highly differentiated organizational structures with significant reductionist tendencies—are charged by society with the task of training competent graduates, conducting research, and providing patient care. The way in which public funds are expended for research and patient care tends to amplify the reductionist tendencies of these centers. In a sense,

society entrusts the training of health care professionals to academic health centers with two contradictory messages. On the one
hand, academic health centers are given the responsibility of training professionals to care holistically for people in the larger society,
implying a belief that the graduates produced will be qualified to
meet the needs of those they will serve. On the other hand, academic health centers are given significant incentives (funding and
autonomy) to train students, conduct research, and provide patient
care in ways that promote reductionism and differentiation.

The involvement of academic health centers is a critical link in
the seven Community Partnerships. The primacy of these centers
in health professions education requires their partnership and active
participation in this effort. A major goal of the Community Partnerships initiative is to foster change in academic health center
structures—although as organizations they tend to resist adaptation—to support a sustained increase in the number of suitably educated primary care practitioners to meet the needs of communities.
To that end, the seven Community Partnerships have developed
assorted strategies for enhancing interaction with communities and
creating a climate in which power can be shared.

For the Community Partnerships, and for academic health centers, power takes many forms. In academic health centers, power
may be seen as influence over internal policy matters such as budget and expenditures or as control over research subjects, curriculum, student time, and methods of assessment. It is in these defining
areas—internal policy, curriculum, student time, and so on—that
the Community Partnerships require academic health centers to
share the power they hold. Each Partnership's linking structure is
the primary mechanism for this sharing. Through this structure, the
influences that shape health professions education are expanded by
linking academic health centers with the communities they serve.
For the academic health centers participating in Community Partnerships, then, the question becomes, How much power is an established institution prepared to give a new linking organization that
it does not control?

Power sharing is very difficult for any organization; it is certainly difficult for the academic health center. The purpose of such a center is only the sum of its departments' purposes. An academic health center's purpose is not vested, in any collective sense, in the total organization; it lies only in its various parts. With the school of medicine separated from the schools of nursing, pharmacy, dentistry, and social work, the only collective activity they share may be rooting for the same football team. And within each school—within medicine and nursing, dentistry, social work, and public health— the department structure supports even greater separateness. Individual departments have the power to control faculty careers, promotion and tenure, research grants, and patient care revenues. In light of this internal fragmentation of power, sharing power with the community is all the more difficult. After all, none of these differentiated organizational bodies of expertise shares anything with the others.

Power sharing with communities brings additional difficulties. Philosophically and functionally, society has granted our institutions of higher learning the responsibility to educate qualified graduates and to generate and preserve knowledge. Universities grant degrees, and in carrying out this degree-granting responsibility, institutions turn to their experts (the faculty) to set standards (curricula and courses) and determine whether graduates have met those standards (student assessment). All of this is captured in a simple but profound sentence routinely intoned by the university president at commencement: "By the authority vested in me by the university board of trustees and upon recommendation of the faculty, I hereby bestow upon you the degree of _____."

The Community Partnerships initiative acknowledges both the fundamental educational obligation that society vests in universities and the societal expectation that academic health centers be more responsive to the needs of people. For this reason, the seven Partnerships have been challenged to create structures that both preserve the institutional educational role and increase accountability.

Academic Health Centers and the Community Partnerships

The task of examining the extent to which different Community Partnerships have been able to share power and determining where power rests with each Partnership underscores the challenge of this linking process and instructs others who may seek to adapt health professions training to community needs. In Figure 5.1, the seven Partnerships are considered against two major dimensions of power manifested through this change process.

Along the *horizontal axis* is the relative degree to which an academic health center shares power (influence/involvement) with regard to educational, financial, and research policies. Does the power to direct policy, curriculum, student time, faculty activity, and resources rest with the community, the new linking structure, or the academic health center?

On the *vertical axis* are the three most prominent categories of formal organizational structure. Among each of the seven sites, does

Figure 5.1. Community Partnerships and the Locus of Power.

ORGANIZATIONAL FORMALIZATION	LOCUS OF POWER		
	Community	Community Partnership	Academic Health Center
Incorporated or Other Legal Entity			**XX**
Independent but Not Legally Able to Receive Funds		**XX**	
Advisory to Another Organization		**XX**	**X**

Each x represents a CP/HPE site.

the Community Partnership structure function as an advisory body only, does it have some formal structure short of incorporation, or is it autonomous and incorporated?

As indicated in the figure, none of the seven Community Partnerships is community controlled, in spite of the fact that six of the seven projects have a majority of community representation on Partnership boards. Three of the seven Partnerships are dominated by academic health centers. The two formally incorporated Partnership structures fall into this category. Although one might expect that such a high degree of formality in an organizational structure would suggest a correspondingly high level of community involvement, in this case it does not.

Four of the seven Partnerships, however, have invested the Partnership structure with some power. To varying degrees, the shift of the locus of power from academic health centers to the Partnership structure indicates that the Community Partnerships exert some influence over student experiences and time, budget, faculty activities and rewards, curricular changes, and/or institutional policy.

The type of support provided by communities and academic health centers tells more about the extent to which power has been shared to date. Although communities have had relatively little power and resources to share, the in-kind support they have provided the Partnerships (support in the form of buildings and land) is substantial, indicative of an enduring commitment. Academic health centers, by contrast, have in general provided more tentative support—they have loaned personnel, for instance—which may point to a weaker commitment to the Partnerships.

The Community Partnerships initiative posits as the desired structure an independent, incorporated organizational body through which communities and academic health centers can share power, create a common transcending mission, and increase the relevance of the activities of academic health centers to the needs of people. The creation of such a viable, boundary-spanning organizational structure to which power is given would be the means whereby academic health centers can be encouraged to adapt. However, none of the seven Partnerships has achieved this goal in three and one-half years of work.[1] The question, of course, is "Why not?"

Some Lessons Learned About Academic Health Centers

As can be seen in the right-hand column of Figure 5.1, three of the Community Partnerships are still dominated by academic health centers. These Partnerships, along with the other four, provide valuable lessons about academic health centers. The lessons include the following:

• For any organization, sharing power is extremely difficult. For an organization as differentiated as an academic health center, sharing power is generally even more difficult. By design, society grants academe—and academe, in turn, grants faculty—the prerogative and responsibility of ensuring that its graduates are competent. Competency, in this regard, is in the eye of the beholder, however. Faculty—who control the course of curriculum, define research questions, and pursue data collection to support that research— guard their traditional prerogatives closely. Giving community representatives, or any kind of organizational structure within or outside the university, a legitimate voice in the decisions faculty have always made is difficult indeed.

• Creating a formal organizational structure to share in what academic health centers have been doing on their own for years raises an often-heard question from the academic health center side of some Partnerships: Why do we need it? The answer, of course, is that the organizational structure is needed only if the academic health center wants to link with communities and to become

---

[1]Recently one Partnership advisory board did make the decision to incorporate, but it is too early to determine what impact this development may have on the Partnership over the long term.

responsive and directly accountable to parties other than funding sources. If the primary intent of the academic health center is to maintain the status quo, there may be no need for a linking organizational structure.

• Academic health center leaders are afraid of linking their institutions with communities because they perceive that their own futures may be tied more closely to the collective opinions of department heads and faculty inside of their institutions than to the viewpoints of community representation from outside it.

• By the same token, universities, like all organizations, tend to want to control their public image and lobbying agenda. Linking with one or more outside organizational structures is perceived as reducing rather than increasing influence. In general, academic health centers and their faculty seek to gain increased control of resources (or at the very least to maintain the status quo).

• There are no established linking organizational structures except those mandated by an external force. This force, as in the case of the Community Partnerships projects, may be an entity that mandates a linking structure as a condition for obtaining funds for support. Other entities, however, such as local, state, or federal governmental bodies, may mandate the creation of managerial organizational structures to handle relatively routine matters—monthly budget reports and the creation of personnel policies, for example.

• In addition to an absence of linking structures in academic health centers, there is an absence of leadership. Even when an academic leader recognizes the need for a new organizational structure, it takes an enormous amount of time, commitment, and patience to help create it.

In spite of these significant challenges, some academic health centers have moved to share power with communities through viable Partnership organizational structures. In four of these, academic health centers have given a significant amount of power over their activities to these developing structures.

Two considerations may guide an academic health center's involvement in creating a new organizational structure. First, university-wide and academic leadership at the school or department level may realize that leading academic institutions in the direction of increasing their societal contribution requires them to work from the outside in. Creating boundary-spanning organizational structures is a means to achieving this end. Second, there is a difference between the short- and long-term perspectives. In the short run, creating a boundary-spanning organizational structure and orchestrating its capacity to make demands upon an academic institution may unnecessarily compromise the academic health center's income-generating capabilities. In the long term, however, increasing community involvement and support for the work of academic health centers will lead to sustained financial support through the policy-making process.

In sum, the organizational characteristics and dynamics of academic health centers may be quite separate from the intentions (often good) of those who work in these institutions and hold apparent positions of influence.

- Academic health centers, like all organizations, are driven by the desire for self-preservation. To this end, they seek to please those outside the organization who provide funds to sustain their activities and those inside who have influence over organizational practices.

- Academic health centers, like all organizations, perceive the sharing of power as a loss of control over their destiny and ability to survive.

- Academic health centers, like all organizations (but especially those composed of professionals), tend to differentiate into smaller and smaller groups of expertise, always working toward the perceived ideal of individual autonomy for the expert faculty member.

These characteristics affect the likelihood that an academic health center will link successfully with the community. Although the academic health centers of the Community Partnerships exhibit these characteristics, in some cases their influences have been tempered by other considerations. For example, the relative dependence of an academic health center on the interests of the community it serves may act as a constraint on these dynamics. Likewise, the historical mission of the institution—its relative balance between teaching, research, and patient care; its focus on either high-tech or primary care; its status as a private or public institution; the scope of its sense of mission and purpose (regional, state, or national)—may serve to blunt the organizational tendencies of academic health centers.

Some of the academic health centers associated with the Community Partnerships initiative have moved to share power with communities through viable Community Partnerships. In some cases, academic health centers have been led to create such power-sharing linkages with departmental leadership and faculty fully aware of the potential long-term benefits of the Partnership. In others, academic health centers have moved more reluctantly, without leadership and faculty understanding the implications of the adaptation. In all seven Community Partnerships, the dynamics of the community and the development of the specific linking organizational structure heavily impinge on the success of this power-sharing attempt. Chapters Six and Seven examine the role of these forces in greater detail.

6

. . . .

The Nature of Communities

Bruce Behringer and Ronald W. Richards

Figure 6.1, repeated from the previous chapter, places the seven Community Partnerships in one of three "locus of power" columns—community, Community Partnership, or academic health center—indicating the primary source of the new organizational structure's power. The column on the left, labeled *community*, is curiously empty. None of the seven Partnership organizations appears to derive its power from the community it serves—in spite of the fact that the Kellogg Foundation initiative is entitled Community Partnerships with Health Professions Education. This raises some interesting and important questions: Why are there no projects in which the power is controlled by the community? What is the nature of the power, if any, that the community holds? What is the rationale for the community's involvement in the Community Partnerships model?

The first of these questions was answered earlier in this book. Education of health professionals has never been the domain of communities. Our society delegates operational responsibility for all types of education to experts; in addition, it delegates control over this process, to a greater or lesser degree, to institutions made up of experts. In some cases, communities retain fairly active control over educational systems. Public school systems, for example— the systems of experts responsible for training our children—are controlled by school boards made up of community members and

Figure 6.1. Community Partnerships and the Locus of Power.

		LOCUS OF POWER		
ORGANIZATIONAL FORMALIZATION		Community	Community Partnership	Academic Health Center
	Incorporated or Other Legal Entity			**XX**
	Independent but Not Legally Able to Receive Funds		**XX**	
	Advisory to Another Organization		**XX**	**X**

Each *x* represents a CP/HPE site.

by voters who approve or deny millages. Through these mecha-nisms, community control of public school systems extends to cur-riculum, policy, budget, system design, faculty composition, allocation of funds for building construction or renovation, and other areas of operations.

Although communities are active in the administration of pub-lic school systems, their level of involvement with higher educa-tion, particularly health professions education, is minimal. Communities have almost no functional control over universities and academic health centers. What students are taught, how they are taught, how the funds allocated to support health professions education are spent—these concerns are traditionally outside the realm of communities.

Communities likewise exercise little direct control over the allo-cation of funding to universities and academic health centers. In theory, at least, communities are represented in the legislative process at the state and federal levels. Through this mechanism, funds are continually designated to support institutional activities. In reality, however, communities have lost control over how much, and in what ways, tax dollars are spent on the education of health professionals. The complexity of the allocation process contributes in large part to this lack of involvement. The complexity of the legislative process presents another hurdle: communities—and those who represent their interests—have not the time, knowledge, or resources to fully participate in that process. They are certainly no match for the lobbyists representing the various interest groups committed to either preserving the status quo or modifying it to their advantage. Given the complexity of the system, communities are little able to participate in the legislative and funding processes that impact the education of health professionals.

If they choose to recognize and exercise it, however, communities have considerable power to exert. For example, communities have the power to influence the legislative process and could, if they chose, affect the allocation of funds to academic health centers. Communities also have the power to control certain kinds of resources—space in a church building or land at a public school site—that could have an impact on how and where health professionals are educated.

Communities have significant resources of this kind and contribute them to the Community Partnerships initiative. But the allocation of such community resources is very difficult to coordinate. Communities are loose coalitions of interest groups that periodically fuse to accomplish a common goal. Working together, these coalitions are able to benefit the wider community and create a win-win situation for their constituencies. But communities, like academic health centers, find it hard to share the power they hold. In some Community Partnerships, communities share the power they have; in others, they do not.

There are advantages to participating in the Community Partnerships, however, that may be shared by both academic health centers and communities—advantages that override the parochial interests of each. Community involvement in educating health professionals, for instance, may provide communities with a more ready supply of health professionals to meet the needs of community members: the students who train within a community may be more inclined to practice there when training is completed. Community involvement in health professions education may also lead more local young people to pursue health professions careers. These too may eventually serve their home community.

Academic health centers also stand to benefit from the Community Partnership. Educational leaders may find in communities the impetus they need to promote change within their institutions. The outside pressures of what communities need and want from health care providers can foster change inside the institutions training health professionals. And involving communities and community providers in training health professionals brings fresh knowledge and perspective to what is being taught. When the community becomes a place where health professionals are taught, students acquire a very different set of skills. Within the culture of communities, students learn from the perspectives of families. They see firsthand the many conditions that impact health and the ways community people have of managing and surviving among them. Communities teach health professions students things they cannot learn in hospitals, and students are wiser for that experience.

The Dynamics of Community

The concept of *community*—although often referred to—remains a difficult construct to define. Community is not as abstract as the "ideal state" Plato, Rousseau, and Marx described in their writings, nor is it as simple as an area on a map with a set of tangible boundaries (Tinder, 1980). It lies somewhere in between. The concept of community encompasses people in a particular place and time, but it also speaks to their history and language and to the shared meaning that develops where history and language intersect. Essentially, communities are complex webs of people—webs shaped by relationships, interdependence, mutual interests, and patterns of interaction (Taub, 1989).

Communities are organized around the exchange of goods and services, the abundance or scarcity of resources, and the division of labor these conditions require among their members (Nix, 1983). Adaptive communities, Harold L. Nix suggests, recognize their interdependence and seek "an organized approach to compromise and a system of conflict management" (1983, p. 241). But unlike organizations, communities do not depend on structure or hierarchy to coordinate exchanges and manage conflict. Structure may be effective in guiding the development of a corporation, but communities work differently: communities function through collaboration and communication on many levels. Only by balancing the needs and demands of diverse constituencies do they survive. Resilient communities are born of conflict and resolution and renewed conflict—and the trust that springs from these often difficult "births."

Communities are characterized by a fluid dynamism. Community "history" is related in stories rather than data. Community "boundaries" fluctuate with the formation and dissolution of loose coalitions that spring up to address each timely issue. Power among groups and individuals is shared and negotiated depending on issues and needs. Leadership is determined by service, relationships, and an understanding of community values. In the absence of formal structures, informal networks and linkages support the relational glue that binds community interest groups. In the absence of formal position, leaders work through groups of people and their connections.

Professionals, experts, and the institutions they shape seldom see communities in these terms, however. Tom Dewar's tongue-in-cheek description of his early work with a Wisconsin-area agency on aging crystallizes both the professional expert's approach to communities and its limitations:

Being a really well trained, inexperienced sociologist, I designed a very thorough needs analysis because that is what we've been taught you do with communities. You do a needs analysis. So I developed an interview where I could sit down with an older person and, in an hour, identify not only all the things that probably were really wrong, but make the person I was interviewing nervous about several things they weren't even sure were wrong with them. . . . When I reported the results of three months of these interviews to my advisory committee, a couple of older people serving on it weren't impressed by the uniquack babble of modern sociology that had gotten me the job. One said, "Well, Tom, you've told me a lot about what might be wrong with these people—the part of the glass that is empty. But I want to know about the part that is full" [Dewar, 1990, pp. 3–4].

Dewar offers this anecdote as an observation about how professionals tend to conceptualize communities. Communities, he claims, are viewed as prospective or current clients—clients with needs or deficiencies that professional expertise can remedy. Yet when professional "experts" approach communities, their effectiveness is hampered by a number of factors. The community's unease with the expert is one difficulty. And professionals in multiple fields must bridge barriers created by differing language, expertise, and status to connect with communities. But they must also move beyond their own perceptions of communities as essentially "in need." Professionals, Dewar suggests, must abandon the tendency to define communities solely by what they lack.

John McKnight (1986) also urges professionals to abandon this "communities are full of problems" mindset and view communities in terms of the resources they possess. Rather than helping, McKnight contends, programs based on communities' deficits actually do harm. As experts seek to define communities in terms of problems that need a particular expertise to "fix" them, our society loses touch with the rich capability of communities and the people living in them.

Approaches to Community Participation

Although the past thirty years provide examples of a wide range of approaches to involving communities in the development or delivery of programs designed to serve them, few of these approaches have successfully bridged the trust barriers that exist between institutions and communities. Community development and program evaluation literature is replete with descriptions of a continuum of approaches from "manipulation" to "empowerment," all intended to accomplish community participation. Unfortunately, none of these has proved to be *the* solution to involving community.

The term "maximum feasible participation" was coined as part of the War on Poverty programs in the 1960s. To receive the maximum available federal funding, programs were required to seek input from the group being targeted. The intent was to provide an incentive for community participation through governance and to ensure an acceptable entrée to the community for federal dollars. This approach produced a decade of individual and community participation programs operated through community-controlled efforts such as Community Action agencies and Model Cities programs.

Community Action agencies attempted to bypass "city hall"— the structure that federal lawmakers saw as part of the unresponsive milieu that created the need for antipoverty programs. Forming an organization of familiar and trusted community representatives was seen as one way to increase community participation. Model Cities programs, on the other hand, put funds in the hands of local agencies. But, as with Community Action agencies, support hinged on the extent to which programs were developed by and for representatives of communities in poverty. Subsequent programming targeting health issues—Community Health Centers, Health Systems Agencies, Regional Medical Programs—was modeled on this same approach.

In general, the participative direction of federal programming and support laid the groundwork for the "community organization" mentality. To lend credibility to the loose coalitions and networks characteristic of community dynamics, some leaders embraced a "businesslike" approach to participation. Thus "Community Action agencies" paved the way for "community development corporations," which applied corporate-style structure, management, and approaches to community challenges.

Another consequence of these initial forays into required community participation was the emergence of a group of community organizations and leaders who became "participation experts." In the past thirty years, both organizations and individuals have sought to identify themselves as representing the interests of—and links to—"the community." They have claimed the right to represent "community" and have created a new layer of participation between people and programs.

If federal programs of the 1960s and 1970s served to develop "expert" community representatives, they also brought a great many professional "experts"—sociologists, psychologists, economists, nutritionists, health professionals—to community problems. Whether the issue was health, poverty, or education, experts—university-trained professionals—were employed to assess community needs and to develop, implement, and evaluate programs. The questionable efficacy of bringing "experts" to communities—coming, as they generally do, from a very different culture—has not altered this trend in recent years. Despite Dewar's and McKnight's admonitions to view communities in terms of their resources and strengths, community "problems" almost always seem to require services from professional "experts."

Working with Communities

Three decades of community participation efforts with targeted populations, neighborhoods, and communities have had mixed success.

"Maximum feasible participation" has evolved into "empowerment" and "community development," but professional "experts" and community participation "experts" remain the major players. Although the collective work of these participants has not exactly succeeded in reinvigorating public life, at least their experience has taught us some of the pitfalls to placing communities in legitimate positions of influence.

A guiding principle underlying the Community Partnerships initiative (and Kellogg Foundation programming in general) is the belief that community involvement is one critical element of a successful problem-solving approach. This belief—that the problems of people are better addressed if the community is involved—underscores multiple activities funded through the Kellogg Foundation.

The Community Partnerships model has drawn on these principles and the developmental experiences described in preceding paragraphs in crafting its inclusive approach to community involvement. Rather than allowing language, self-interest, and lack of information to separate community people from "experts," the Partnerships have worked to integrate ideas, people, and resources in both development and implementation. In his article describing a collaborative partnership in rural Wisconsin, Tim Size adapts DePree's corporate leadership principles to describe the premises that guide his program's efforts (Size, 1993). The four "rights" that Size describes speak to the Community Partnerships' inclusive approach:

1. *The right to be needed.* People in communities must be approached in terms of their assets. Each partner has unique resources that must be recognized, valued, and employed in addressing health professions education.

2. *The right to be involved.* Local organizations and individuals are sources of expertise and experience within the community. Involving multiple organizations and individuals in health professions education decision making and activities

builds on what community people and their representatives already know and enhances the scope and validity of health professions education.

3. *The right to understand.* People in communities need to understand the "big picture" of health professions education objectives and challenges (economic and policy issues, for example), just as institutions need to understand the dynamics of the "local scene." The flow of information between institutions and communities needs to move both ways, pushing members of both groups beyond the traditional boundaries of their knowledge and understanding.

4. *The right to make a commitment.* Although systems are becoming more complex—and decisions, according to Size, are seen as more impersonal and abstract—communities tend to commit to people rather than institutions. To facilitate this type of commitment, Community Partnerships seek to expand contact and personal involvement among community people and institutional representatives.

Recognition of these "rights" by institutions and their representatives is a beginning. But even with an inclusive approach, some communities will resist taking an active role in this type of collaborative process. Among the Community Partnership communities, some have responded enthusiastically to the opportunity to educate health professionals, while others have held back. Some people in communities have looked for ways to participate in the process, have sought to identify a common vision, and have assumed responsibility for operations and policy issues. Others have expected academic health centers to take the initiative and have waited to be led.

The circumstances that impel communities to coalesce around an opportunity such as the Community Partnerships program are as many and varied as the communities themselves. In some instances, timing and the emergence of local issues bring the strengths of communities to the fore. In others, a critical incident or crisis galvanizes community resources. In still others, an academic institution's willingness to work toward common goals is pivotal. Whatever the form or timing of the catalyst, however, some communities seem to be able to overlook past disappointments and invest their resources in a promising new venture with surprising speed and vigor.

Lessons from the Community Partnerships

Although the full influence of community in the Partnerships continues to develop, four Partnership structures have successfully drawn on community resources to create organizational structures in which power is shared (as the figure presented earlier indicates). In these cases, more community members than academic representatives sit on Partnership boards. The character and activity level of these Partnerships reflect the perspective that community can bring to any endeavor. The related lessons that Community Partnerships provide, outlined briefly below, have bearing on any programming effort seeking to involve the community in efforts intended to serve them.

- *Developing community trust takes time.* Communities are seldom homogeneous or easily accessed. Identifying their diverse constituencies and networks takes time; building sufficient trust to work together is a much longer process. In some instances, communities' previous experiences with institutions may be an additional barrier to trust. Although some communities are willing to move beyond past misunderstandings, creating the trusting climate needed to form a viable partnership takes time. Community Partnerships take the long-term view of seeking community participation, with the understanding that solid relationships form over time and with firsthand experience.
- *Communities must be given a legitimate role in the decision-making process.* In order for communities to exercise the power they have,

academic health centers must be willing to share the power they hold over health professions education. Involving communities in the project budget and other operations concerns, framing key programmatic issues in lay language, and tangibly demonstrating a willingness to work together all contribute to placing communities in a legitimate position to guide and support health professions education.

When communities are provided with the position, the needed information, and the rationale for participating, the level of commitment and involvement they deliver can give a tremendous boost to the project. In those Partnerships with more community than academic representatives serving on boards, evaluators report more discussion and negotiation when goal changes are made, more productive involvement in setting and expanding project goals, a stronger sense of shared vision, greater role clarity, and less role conflict. Communities are very able partners; capable of vigorous participation, they must be encouraged to take a leading role in collaborative efforts.

• *Communities have a great many more resources than they think they have.* Decades of deficit-based needs analysis have affected how communities see themselves, especially in relation to "experts" such as health professionals and university faculty. But when communities are mobilized, their resources—and their contributions of time, space, expertise, contacts, and energy—have made out-of-hospital health professions education viable.

In Partnerships where community board members outnumber academic representatives, evaluators note significant increases in coordinating services and joint projects, expanded information exchange, greater tolerance of differences, and more productive ways of handling conflict. And both community and academic representatives in these Partnerships report greater levels of commitment and satisfaction with their involvement in the project. Communities do more with what they have, and they bring invaluable expertise and experience to every level of a project.

• *Communities are willing to assume responsibility for health professions education.* Although health professions education is traditionally outside their domain and control, communities are willing to become active partners in educating the providers who will serve them in the future. Community members see the investment of time, resources, and energy as an investment in their community and their community's future. With great respect for what they do not know about medicine, nursing, social work, and dentistry, communities take responsibility for the piece of health professions education they *can* deliver—knowledge about what is needed and desired, nontraditional sites for service delivery, local providers to supplement training, and the time, experience, and wide contacts needed to ensure that everything runs smoothly.

• *Community connections with policy makers are often superior to institutional connections, but they are underutilized on behalf of the Community Partnerships.* Communities know their elected officials. Civic and business leaders are often on a first-name basis with their local, state, and federal representatives. Their links with these influential individuals—links based on history, ongoing communication, and mutual interests—can connect the Partnerships with state and federal decision making in a way that institutions cannot. Academic institutions are obligated to work through an organizational structure, but community people can go right to the source—often with surprising results.

Within the Community Partnerships, however, these valuable links with policy makers have not yet been fully realized. Community representatives tend to defer to academe in this arena, despite their superior position. As active participants in the Community Partnerships, communities must work within the partnership structure to develop policy objectives and then mine their contacts accordingly.

• *Communities are often more optimistic partners than institutions.* Because community coalitions and networks are built on relationships, community partners are skilled at maintaining (and reforming) those coalitions when difficult issues divide loyalties. As the Community Partnerships have developed, communities have often taken the lead in teaching educational leaders about trust building and have worked successfully to maintain a cooperative spirit in the face of conflict. In the Partnerships with a majority of community representatives in board service, these team-building skills have produced greater levels of project activity, a more clearly defined vision, greater agreement on project goals, and higher levels of satisfaction among all board participants.

The Community Partnerships initiative has created a mechanism for drawing on the expertise and will of community people to reshape health professions education. In some cases, the initiative has placed the community in a legitimate position to exercise its power over the approach, method, and content of health professions education. The role of the new linking structures in facilitating this balance of power will be explored in the following chapter.

• •

7

Creating New Organizational Structures

Patricia Maguire Meservey and Ronald W. Richards

A t the outset of the Community Partnerships with Health Professions Education initiative, the W.K. Kellogg Foundation mandated "significant community involvement" to bridge the gap between the needs of people and the way health professionals are educated. That mandate grew from the belief that significant involvement by communities could increase the relevance of health professions education to the needs of people and, over time, change the way educational institutions function. To facilitate this community involvement, the projects have developed linking organizations—structures that support and formalize connections between communities and educational institutions and encourage a balance of power between the two.

Figure 7.1, repeated from Chapter Five, examines two dimensions of these structures—the locus of power and the extent of formal organization—as a method of assessing progress toward the model's ideal. Four Community Partnerships have invested their structures with considerable power, but none of these has achieved the level of independence and autonomy that incorporation implies.

This chapter will focus on the four Community Partnerships resting in the center column, weighing what they have to teach about building and nurturing new structures. Content will include the *history* of linking organizations and *factors* that have influenced the development of these four Community Partnerships structures;

Figure 7.1. Community Partnerships and the Locus of Power.

	LOCUS OF POWER		
ORGANIZATIONAL FORMALIZATION	Community	Community Partnership	Academic Health Center
Incorporated or Other Legal Entity			**XX**
Independent but Not Legally Able to Receive Funds		**XX**	
Advisory to Another Organization		**XX**	**X**

Each x represents a CP/HPE site.

it will also identify *what new structures need* to become sustainable based on the collective experience of the Community Partnerships.

Lessons from the Past

The idea of linking communities with institutions is not a new one. It has long been recognized that people are more responsive to activities and services when they have been engaged in planning and decision making. But despite this understanding, few institutions establish successful linkages with communities. It is difficult to balance the interests of academic leaders, who are accustomed to exerting influence in institutions, and community people, who are less experienced in the formal structural ways in which decision making occurs in complex organizations. Power struggles often explain the demise of such efforts. Those who hold organizational power presume that they know the best method of addressing a concern and vigorously resist sharing authority, responsibility, and control with recipients of services. And the mechanisms intended to facilitate the sharing often fall short of the mark. The federal programs initiated in the 1960s, touched on in the previous chapter, provide several examples of this type of difficulty.

War on Poverty programs, including Model Cities, were designed to address community needs with federal funding, structure, and support. The intent of these efforts was to circumvent local authorities and the way they tended to allocate resources. The varying structures required by these programs attempted to strike a balance between autonomy in local planning and implementation and the need for a central force to hold projects together across the country.

Model Cities programs attempted to coordinate local agencies and solicited community input through community decision organizations. These mechanisms were intended to ensure that the community had a voice in planning and implementation, but the overall design of Model Cities muted their influence. Model Cities was a vertical ladder to Washington. The organizational structure was complex and required multiple levels of decision-making review, each farther away from the community of service. The actual power of the community decision organizations was diminished through this structure. It became difficult to determine whether the local citizens were making decisions or were only endorsing decisions made at higher levels. The legitimacy of the community decision organizations also came under fire. In the end, fundamental questions of participation (Who represents the community? How do you define community?), along with diffused decision making and a complex bureaucracy, led to the downfall of the program.

Most of the War on Poverty programs, however, were far more decentralized than Model Cities. Rather than connecting local organizations and agencies to a formal structure that linked to Washington, the War on Poverty's "maximum feasible participation" approach gave individuals and groups considerable control over programming and services. VISTA, Job Corps, Head Start, Upward Bound, and the Neighborhood Youth Corps, all grew from this decentralized approach.

Although born of great excitement and energy, the War on Poverty programs required a tremendous amount of attention and energy. To foster their development, many of the programs were assigned to a new agency—the Office of Economic Opportunity (OEO). Though the newly created office faced opposition at its inception, President Johnson believed that "the best way to kill a new idea is to put it in an old line agency" (Wofford, 1980, p. 295). His instincts, as it turned out, were correct. Of the programs that have survived—Head Start, for instance—many grew to maturity in the new organizational structure of the OEO.

The approach of using governmental resources and influence to circumvent local systems and meet the needs of people also facilitated the creation of community health centers. Developed out of the War on Poverty programs, community health centers were created by federal funds to address the unmet health needs of disadvantaged citizens, bypassing presumed inadequate or inattentive public health systems. Community health centers were administered by boards similar to the Model Cities structures. Most of the health center systems established in the 1960s developed sources of funding beyond federal allocations and still survive today.

While some individual programs—Head Start and community health centers among them—enjoyed some success, the overall lack of administrative structure at the federal level limited what the War on Poverty programs were collectively able to accomplish. The magnitude of the effort, and the varied and ambitious initiatives it spawned, needed more attention than President Johnson's administration was able to deliver. With little coordination at the federal level (by Sargent Shriver's description, "a bunch of Boston Tea parties all over the country" [Wofford, 1980, p. 320]), strong opposition from local authorities, and ongoing struggles for control among local agencies and politicians, the War on Poverty eventually failed to sustain the degree of community involvement that was intended.

Another example of the federal "carrot" approach to change is found in the area health education centers (AHECs). AHECs were federally funded attempts to move academic health centers toward communities. Based on a 1970 Carnegie Commission study that identified unmet needs, AHECs were funded with federal and (later) state dollars, creating alternate systems for educating students and providing services. AHECs accomplished much throughout their history; unfortunately, however, allocations to AHECs were made to medical schools—the very institutions most vested in maintaining the academic health center's status quo.

Although many of these attempts to create organizational structures linking institutions with communities were less than successful, the historical perspective these efforts provide is a significant one. The importance of communities' assuming a major role in decision making, the need for institutions to share power and a common purpose to support a new structure, the necessity of a new entity being independent of old-line structures, the impact of funding that is not tied to existing systems—all of these are lessons taught by well-intentioned programs over the past thirty years.

Academic Community Health Systems

The Community Partnerships have drawn on the historical lessons of early structures and moved beyond them. Local efforts shaped locally join with academic health centers to create organizations through which power can be shared. The Partnerships bring together representatives of community health centers, hospitals, local government, the citizenry, and academic health centers into an organizational structure that in turn has the responsibility of creating and guiding academic, non-hospital-based community health systems. Each of the members of a Partnership lays claim to one or two of the general functions of delivering patient care, conducting research, or educating health professionals. None represents an organization that carries out the education of health professionals in out-of-hospital, community-linked, multidisciplinary settings. That is the distinct role of the linking structure that lies at the heart of each Community Partnership.

Although a product of historical lessons learned, the Partnership linking structures are also the result of the Kellogg Foundation's influence. The Kellogg Foundation took two pivotal steps to facilitate the creation of viable structures: the Foundation mandated that linking structures have significant community involvement and a measure of functional control (such as budget approval) over partnership activities, and the Foundation provided technical support, networking opportunities, and education over time to expand the capacity of these developing organizations.

In many respects, the concept of an academic but out-of-hospital health system, created and operated for educational and research purposes, is not new. In fact, the origins of a teaching hospital are similar. As was noted in an earlier chapter, the teaching hospital was created as a place to model the best care possible so that students would learn about such care and how to deliver it; it was also created to provide a place to conduct research to expand our knowledge base and adapt care accordingly. Sharing those same goals, academic community health systems can be characterized as follows:

- They undertake equal responsibility for service, teaching, and research.

- They are community-driven.

- They are partnerships between communities and academic health systems.

- They provide comprehensive health services that are multidisciplinary, preventive, and early-intervention-focused.

- They undertake research that is community-responsive and meets the highest standards of scholarship.

- They undertake a major responsibility for teaching and learning in out-of-hospital settings.

These characteristics of academic community health systems represent the goals of the Partnership linking structures—new structures created to develop and manage new systems of care, teaching, and research within the community.

What New Structures Need

When Patricia Castiglia, dean of the College of Nursing and Allied Health at the University of Texas, El Paso, describes the early negotiations surrounding the development of that area's Partnership organization, she identifies two key requirements for getting off to a good start: a big round table and plenty of chairs. A *round* table, she says, puts academe and community on equal footing from the beginning and keeps each participant in eye contact with others throughout the discussion; and a *big* table with plenty of extra chairs suggests that the Partnership is an accommodating, somewhat elastic group—one not limited to a set number of participants.

To balance the playing field between academic institutions and communities, Community Partnerships form organizational structures. We charge these structures not only with collaborating to develop a new approach to health professions education and primary care delivery but also with creating an environment for sustaining these activities while increasing the number of primary care students their programs produce. Little things—such as the right table and lots of extra chairs—may seem irrelevant in the larger picture, but they are metaphors for successful collaboration. Such metaphors suggest who comes to the table, for what purpose, and what those players contribute to the success of the new structure. How and why these linking organizations are formed—and what tools we provide them to fulfill their charge—affect how viable they become.

The timing of the collaboration is important in the success of negotiations and the rate of implementation of each project. Part-nerships must be formed from the start of the work, incorporating diverse views into the basic philosophy of the project. The rela-tionships between the universities and communities in the seven existing Community Partnerships were not as strong at the outset of the initiative as they are now. There were numerous failed col-laborations, programs begun and not completed, and a sense of com-munities being "used" by academic institutions.

By requiring legitimate community participation from the begin-ning, the initiative helped the Community Partnerships achieve a growth of ideals through a collaborative process. The Partnerships incorporated a process for open dialogue at the outset and have felt continual pressure from the funding agency to continue the dialogue despite periods of impasse.

Power and autonomy are the primary tools for building new organizational structures. Both are necessary for producing and sus-taining an organization that successfully links community with in-stitutions. Autonomy is a big step toward power sharing, but autonomy alone will not ensure that power sharing occurs. The two Partnerships placed in the upper box of the right-hand column of Figure 7.1 have the autonomy that an incorporated structure affords. But these structures are dominated by academe. To achieve a col-laborative relationship, the leadership of both community organi-zations and academic institutions must be ready, willing, and able to share the power they hold with the new structure to ensure its full development. Such is the case with the four Community Part-nerships depicted in the lower two-thirds of the center column. The question related to these latter structures is whether they have or can get the autonomy and authority needed to become sustaining organizational entities.

Thus far, the collective experience of the Community Partner-ships suggests that there are five characteristics that are necessary in the new linking structures if community and academe are to share power and if the linking structures are to achieve autonomy:

1. A collective vision for the new structure

2. Strong leadership

3. Effective managerial systems

4. Control over resources

5. A power base from which to operate

The four Partnership structures in the center column of Figure 7.1 possess each of these elements to some degree. The importance of these factors and their implications for others seeking to establish and nurture new linking structures bear closer examination.

Vision

At the outset of the Kellogg Foundation initiative, each prospective Community Partnership shared a common objective: to secure funding. To meet this objective, community and institutional partners at each site needed to be able to articulate a collective goal in the grant application. In one case, the goal was to reopen a rural hospital. In another, the intent was to place more students from local communities in health professions educational institutions. In a third instance, the impetus was to respond to political demands by state government to make sure that health professions education was aimed at producing rural health providers.

Each Partnership had something tangible that participants wanted to accomplish—something concrete that met the needs of its participants at the inception of the project. But for some new linking structures, once the grant was received and (in some cases) the original objective met, the lack of common purpose became glaringly obvious. Once funds were secured and the hospital was reopened or the need for rural health providers underscored, the gap between the interests of various institutional and community partners took center stage. Neither the academic health centers associated with the Community Partnerships nor the representatives of community groups were prepared to relinquish power and autonomy to a fledgling organization created, more or less, by a private foundation's interest and funding.

Academe and communities bring different priorities to the Partnerships. And the communication habits, language, and cultural perspectives of each, as stated earlier, present natural barriers to true partnership. At first glance, the interests of academic health centers (to educate health professions students, conduct research, and provide services) and communities (to increase the availability of comprehensive health services) seem to blend. But the substantial grant funding that the Community Partnerships receive may have deferred tensions that more limited resources would have uncovered. When resources are few, fundamental questions (such as, Should this program continue to exist; and if so, why?) emerge very early.

Although participants at each of the sites have been working together for more than three years, differing perceptions about project goals have hampered the development of some structures. Some Partnerships, for example, still have no shared vision beyond the early objective. Others have a vision, but it is one determined by the more influential force in the Partnership (an academic health center or an influential community organization, for example) rather than one common to all partners. Without a shared vision, these structures are vulnerable to conflicting influences and are ill-equipped for long-term sustainability.

The four Community Partnerships structures that have achieved some apparent influence and permanency, however, have established a collective sense of purpose beyond the immediate interests of the partners. Within these structures, participants see the mission of the Community Partnership as different from the mission of the organization or group they represent. The vision these partners hold of the Partnership sustains the linking structure and fosters long-term thinking to overcome short-term stumbling blocks.

Given the often conflicting orientation of academic and community partners, however, the visions of these Community Partnership organizations are frequently revisited, particularly as the issue of long-term financial viability looms larger and larger.

Program goals and the visions that sustain them are an ongoing subject of discussion and semantic scrutiny. Partners seem to need to redefine, reassess, and reaffirm their priorities—to clarify the mission and eventually crystallize the vision in their minds. This process of committing and recommitting to the Partnership makes the common vision "real" to those actualizing it and lays a foundation of understanding to support the new organizational structure.

Leadership

Leadership has a pivotal role in the success of the new linking organization. At both board and staff levels, it is an important factor in the development and influence of organizational structures. (The final chapter addresses the role of leadership in greater detail.)

Among the four Partnership organizations in the center column of Figure 7.1, collective leadership has been a patient influence guiding new structures from infancy to tentative first steps and beyond.

Board members in these Partnerships come from academic institutions, community health centers, and community groups. Some are community volunteers and activists; others are on staff at health centers or on faculty at universities or colleges. More than 60 percent of board members serve in that function as unpaid volunteers, yet they not only attend scheduled board meetings but often put in time at a variety of other Partnership activities.

Board members who are able to bridge the cultures of community and academe have secured power and autonomy for Community Partnership linking structures. Whether they represent institutions or community groups, these leaders seek to create a climate of openness within the Partnership structures. Rather than focusing on narrow concerns specific to a particular institution, discipline, or constituency, these board members vigorously engage in clarifying the project vision and then direct their efforts toward making it viable through the structure's operations.

Board members who exert this type of leadership respect the anxiety that abandoning old ways engenders, but they work toward developing a high level of understanding and trust to enable the new organization to take the risk that change requires. They employ all of their expertise, experiences, and interpersonal skills to facilitate productive interaction among group members, guard against premature judgments, and seek consensus. They strive for a neutrality for the collective board. This type of leadership among board members anchors new organizational structures.

Newly formed entities are also built and sustained by the leadership skills of the individual at the helm of the new structure—usually its executive director. The type of leadership most successful in this role, as in other board roles, spans the cultures of community and academe. The varied interpersonal and management skills that contribute to effective participation at the board level are needed here as well. And the ability to create an environment where new territory can be safely charted may be even more valuable in the director's role. However, the difficulty a new organization has in attracting top-notch leadership is significant.

A newly formed structure—especially one created with outside funds available for a specific period of time—is often considered temporary, expected to last only as long as grant money is there to sustain it. Able managers with experience and skill may not view heading a new and possibly transient organization as a step up on the career ladder. Add to this the task of challenging and persuading those who hold power within institutions to share it, as the model requires, and even risk-taking managers may view the demands of the position as too daunting to undertake.

Attracting high-quality leadership—at the board and staff levels—is critical to the success of a new organization, however. The collective leadership of a new structure is its defining asset. It must be cultivated, preserved, and, as circumstances permit, strengthened.

Managerial Systems

New organizations are not grown on vision and leadership alone. These intangible elements must go hand in hand with workable systems and infrastructure to develop a successful organization.

President Johnson's belief about old-line structures notwith-standing, the practical difficulties of setting up a new organizational "home" for an infant project or program often lead to "temporarily" housing it within an existing school or department. In two of the Community Partnerships, for example, the complexity of estab-lishing new systems for employment, benefits, and liability insur-ance was cited as the reason for *not* creating an independent organizational structure. The challenges of developing personnel policies, accounting systems, and a mechanism for accomplishing staff work for board decisions may be overwhelming to a new struc-ture. Furthermore, existing institutions are often hesitant to relin-quish control over budget, staff, and other operations concerns to a new organization.

But a new organization needs to assume a life of its own as soon as possible. Having independent, well-ordered managerial systems in place allows a new organization to attract and retain talented staff. Adequate operations systems allow staff and board leadership to focus energy and attention on the mission of the project. With systems in place, a new organization is positioned to assume a cen-tral role in the work of the program or project it must guide.

Control over Resources

Just as a new program is more likely to thrive if it is part of a new organizational structure, a newly formed entity is more likely to be taken seriously if it has control over its resources.

No organization can last very long if it is dependent on the goodwill of other organizations for its funding. Along with inde-pendent managerial systems, a new organizational structure bene-fits from autonomy in key areas such as resource control and allocation. Without something as basic as budget approval, new organizational structures have no real influence in determining the course of organizational priorities and activities. Yet in the forma-tion of Community Partnership organizations, some academic insti-tutions and community organizations—the partners who came together to seek grant funds—resisted giving these new structures the necessary autonomy to assume control of resources and their allocation.

If new organizations are to reach the level of autonomy necessary to pursue project goals, they need the independence to control a wide variety of functional operations, including the allocation of resources.

Power Base

Viable organizational structures require a power base from which to negotiate. Among the Community Partnerships, power comes from assorted sources—community linkages, local service providers, community need or circumstances, the impetus of a timely political issue. But all four of the structures with some degree of autonomy and power have established both a base from which to operate and further project goals.

- Two Partnership organizations draw their power from the interest and active involvement of the community. In one of these Community Partnerships, the organization has worked to inform the community about the process of state funding allocations to health professions education schools, for example. By empowering the community with knowledge about a complex legislative process and how community members can impact it, the Partnership has gained a potent ally.

- Another Partnership organization's power base is a network of community health centers. Community health centers in this urban site are a source of patient referrals to hospitals. By acting collectively and collaborating with the Community Partnership program, the community health centers create a power base from which the project is able to negotiate with academic health centers.

- A fourth Partnership derives its power base from the state government. Because the state government in this rural site requires medical and nursing schools to cooperate with the Community Partnership organization to qualify for state appropriations, the Partnership organization has considerable influence.

The results of these Community Partnership linkages can be captured in two global descriptions. The first is an organization where clearly separate agencies or communities are joined for a common purpose. Joint decision making is exercised for the areas of work directly related to the task at hand, generally arenas of collaboration that have been predetermined. Each agency retains full rights of autonomy for the tasks that fall within its domain, however, and individual organizational needs often outweigh the needs of the federation. Collaborators represent their separate organizations; they seek not the optimum outcomes for the new organization but the greatest gain for their own individual groups. This more fragile type of organization often raises concerns of conflict of interest and about the long-term survival of the new initiative.

The second model is a true partnership. In this model, there is an increased sense of the whole. Individual organizations have variable levels of power, based on the size, role, or resources that each organization brings to the partnership. There is a strong effort toward joint decision making around issues that affect the whole, leading the partnership toward a clear definition of purpose.

A partnership is an integrative model. It relies on a sharing process in which everyone gives and everyone gains. Trust becomes the cement of the partnership, with each agency's representatives working hard to sustain it. Identity is defined as a whole rather than as separate organizations working collectively. This yields decision making that considers the partnership needs as well as the needs of the individual organizations. Through this type of organization, the playing field is leveled, joint decision making encompasses all aspects of the partnership, and power is shared with true collaboration.

Whatever the source, new linking structures need a power base to be successful. The goodwill of individuals, groups, and institutions may support a project during its early stages; to sustain power sharing over the long term, however, structures need a power base to support their position.

Linking structures seek to put communities and academic institutions on an equal footing, allowing them to work toward common goals, combine their resources, and learn from one another. Although many coalitions are sparked by common interest, mutual need, and available funds, linking organizations need more to be successful. A shared vision, collective leadership, effective managerial systems, control over resources, and a viable power base— these five factors have influenced the development of Community Partnerships structures in the first three years of the initiative.

8

$\cdots\cdots\cdots\cdots\cdots\cdots\cdots\cdots\cdots\cdots\cdots\cdots\cdots\cdots$

How Public Funds Are Spent

Henry A. Foley

A s addressed in Chapter Four, success at reforming health professions education depends upon attending to the external public policy environment. Since the 1970s, various attempts to bring about change in health professions education have been initiated. Although curriculum committees of academic health centers and medical schools have deliberated at length about expectations for students and the content of classes, most medical curricula are a function of financing more than anything else.

The operating budgets of medical schools are predominantly a combination of research funds and money earned by clinical faculty in providing patient care. Most clinical education is paid for by graduate medical education (GME) funds that go directly to teaching hospitals. Our Community Partnerships tell us that most representatives of communities do not understand this process. They presume that tuition and state appropriations cover costs. They also believe that the primary mission of academic health centers is student training. While such presumptions are understandable in the absence of complete information, they are inaccurate.

Even for those with more knowledge about the funding process, the money flow is confusing. Medical school deans, for example, understand that their schools are dependent on GME funding, but few know how much money a hospital in their system receives for graduate medical education.

Other health professions besides medicine tend to be left out of GME, patient care, and research sources of operating income. As the public assumes, they do depend heavily on tuition and state appropriations for their income.

Because the nature of medical education and the nature of academic health centers is so reliant on practice income, research funding, and GME dollars, an understanding of those funding sources is crucial to educational reform efforts. A close look at the way medical education is financed, the impact funding has on health professions education, and the implications of funding for long-term system change provides guidance for those seeking educational reform.

The Funding of Graduate Medical Education

GME financing funds the training of physicians for specific careers they wish to pursue after their undergraduate education. Composed of funding for two types of expenditures, direct and indirect, it comes primarily from Medicare and other insurance. Direct expenditures include those covering the costs for the resident and the physician supervising that resident, and indirect expenditures include all the overhead costs that a hospital can apportion to its residency training.

To support teaching activities, teaching hospitals bill a portion of the administrative costs of these expenditures to Medicare—part of the U.S. Health Care Financing Administration—which uses a formula to negotiate a schedule covering each hospital.

The financing of graduate medical education has been built on the entrepreneurial abilities of hospital administrators, who promote particular hospital-based specialties to create graduate medical programs. Offering enhanced specialty services, hospitals have been able to attract customers with varied medical diagnoses, thus generating revenue for plant maintenance and expansion, staff, and administration.

About 50 percent of GME funding has typically come from Medicare; Medicaid (in some states), the Department of Defense, the Department of Veterans Affairs, and private insurers have also contributed to GME growth. As I have noted, Medicare's subsidies to assist hospitals in training residents include both direct and indirect assistance.

Through direct medical education (DME) payments, teaching hospitals are compensated for each resident trained by the hospital based on the institution's direct costs of training new doctors and the proportion of patient days paid by Medicare. This contribution is not insubstantial, amounting to nearly $1.8 billion a year—17.6 percent of the total funding for graduate medical education. These direct payments help pay for residents' salaries and benefits (about 55 percent of DME dollars), faculty time (26 percent), and other education costs, such as classrooms and laboratory expenses (19 percent) (Alliance for Health Reform, 1994).

Medicare pays teaching hospitals an even greater subsidy for patient care: funds for indirect medical education (IME) expenses amount to more than $4 billion a year, or 31.6 percent of the total cost of graduate medical education. These indirect payments are in recognition of the fact that it is more costly to operate teaching hospitals than community hospitals (because the former involve residents in patient care, have generally sicker patients with less insurance coverage, and pursue more costly interventions in patient care).

How GME Funding Developed

When Medicare was passed into law in 1965, policy makers thought it reasonable to cover the teaching costs associated with the treatment of the older and disabled population through its reimbursement system. It can be argued that they perceived graduate medical education as a collective good and relatively not too expensive at that time. Formulas were derived to reimburse for the teaching costs. As hospital administrators discovered that greater reimbursement accrued to those hospitals that had graduate specialty programs, and that institutions were more marketable with these programs, the number of specialty programs proliferated.

In 1983, Congress established a prospective payment system tying Medicare reimbursement to diagnosis-related groupings (DRGs). Later that year, under pressure from leaders in medical education, Congress exempted GME financing from this payment limitation. Congress created this exemption despite the fact that in 1980 the Graduate Medical Education National Advisory Committee (GMENAC) had reported to Congress, which funded its extensive body of data and analysis, that such a system carried dangers of overproduction of specialists. GMENAC pointed out that an excessive number of specialists could lead to unnecessary procedures performed on the patient population and cautioned that there were not enough potential patients for so many specialists to maintain their skill levels (Graduate Medical Education National Advisory Committee, 1980). Seven years later, the House of Delegates of the American Medical Association agreed with GMENAC that there was an overproduction of specialists. Thus an unintended consequence of this federal policy—that is, the move toward prospective payment—was the further proliferation of programs and consequent acceleration in the growth of the number of specialists.

The leadership of the academic health centers and the deans of medicine (through the Association of American Medical Colleges [AAMC]) effectively lobbied their senators and congressional representatives to enhance the Medicare formulas over a period of fifteen years (1975–1990). The members of the Accreditation Council for Graduate Medical Education—the American Medical Association, the American Association of Medical Colleges, the Council of Medical Specialty Societies, the American Board of Medical Specialties, and the American Hospital Association—lobbied the federal government (specifically, the Health Care Financing Administration) to pay the teaching costs tied to a "reasonable cost" schedule that was heavily skewed to paying for specialty care rather than primary care.

Thus the medical oligopoly shaped a clinical reimbursement system favoring procedural specialties over the so-called cognitive specialties. A major result of this formulation was the skewing of faculty practice plans—the fastest-growing source of support of medical schools and academic health centers—away from primary care and toward subspecialties. The clinical chairpersons in the academic health centers acquired the major role in most practice plans, because they gained more income from their specialty-driven departments than from their other departments. Consequently, specialty residencies became more attractive to undergraduate physicians and hospital administrators than primary care residencies (Solloway, Weiss, and Fagan, 1994).

As fewer students gravitated to primary care, hospitals lost any incentive they might have had to expand family practice and general internal medicine residencies to community-based sites outside the hospitals. The production of specialists became important to those hospitals that wanted to garner greater levels of reimbursement from Medicare and most insurers; it also helped enhance a hospital's prestige. Furthermore, larger reimbursements helped departments in schools of medicine support their increased numbers of professors and improve overhead. By 1992, the total revenue flowing into medical schools from all sources was $23 billion (Jolly and Hudley, 1994).

The dangers of overproduction of specialists and hospital-based curricula were ignored throughout this period of evolution. The production factor in American medical education was out of control.

The supreme irony was that the medical leadership of this period was training many board-certified specialists who left academic health centers and teaching hospitals for community hospitals, where they became competitive enough to offer their services to insurance and managed-care companies at much lower costs. Lately, these payer organizations have been eager to contract with community hospitals and in some markets have canceled many of their contracts with teaching hospitals.

By 1994, the rapid evolution in this country to managed care, with its reduced need for specialists, led to the market reality that the supply of specialists would outstrip the overall requirement for them by 30 percent (or 165,000 physicians) before the end of the decade. Indeed, data suggested that while the aggregate production of primary care physicians was adequate, their distribution was not: not enough of them were attracted to rural areas (Weiner, 1993).

This view may have been premature, however, because managed-care organizations are increasingly bidding for rural as well as urban areas. It is likely that they will take advantage of the surplus of specialists, retraining some of them for practice (perhaps in teams with physician assistants and nurses) in these rural areas.

The emphasis on hospital-based training in recent decades has had mixed results. Physicians graduating from their residencies are highly skilled at determining underlying organic diseases, if they exist, and at using very sophisticated technology for diagnostic and surgical procedures, both in their offices and in the hospital setting. And they are extremely well paid for their procedure-driven specialties.

Physicians have not been taught utilization consciousness in medical school and graduate work, however. They have been trained to have a low tolerance for uncertainty, and as a consequence tend to order all possible tests even when delay would not compromise care. They are ill-equipped to handle pressure from patients for unnecessary studies, procedures, and drugs. They are used to reimbursement of procedures, not patient management. By and large, they have not been taught that health care is a service industry (as police and fire services are) with accountability to society or that care should be delivered by a team; they are not aware that they must deal with biopsychosocial as well as organizational factors.

Physicians in general are ill-equipped for managed-care environments. The Group Health Association of America (GHAA), which represents HMOs, has reported that a large proportion of physicians recruited to managed-care plans are ill-prepared clinically, economically, and/or personally to work in that environment. For example, physicians under capitated contracts can go broke simply because they do not recognize when they are providing unnecessary care (Boland, 1993).

GME financing is clustered in eight states—New York, Massachusetts, Texas, California, Pennsylvania, Ohio, Michigan, and Maryland—which represent more than 50 percent of the total (Garg, Boex, Davis, and Rodos, 1993). The congressional delegations of these states use an enormous amount of leverage to preserve the GME funding through Medicare, and they recently attempted to expand the total amount. By 1994, the year of health reform, GME had become "political pork." In that summer, the academic lobbyists, through their congressional allies, advocated additional billions for graduate medical education despite an estimated excess of 140,000 to 165,000 specialists in the United States (Kosterlitz, 1994). The AAMC endorsed a version of health care reform that included designated funding for graduate medical education, academic health centers, and medical schools to total $68 billion by 2001. Its president noted in his August letter to the Senate that the funding accounts "will provide the financial stability necessary to assure that the education and research missions of our nation's medical schools and teaching hospitals will continue to flourish and meet the needs of the American people" (Cohen, 1994a, p. 5).

What does this brief history of GME funding tell us? When Congress created Medicare, building in provisions for the payment of graduate medical education, specialists were increasing (in number and type) due to funding by the National Institutes of Health (NIH), the Department of Defense, and the Veterans Administration and to increased expectations from American consumers (Ginzberg, 1990). When GMENAC acknowledged in 1980 that there was an overproduction of specialists in most fields—one that would only increase—Congress and the medical complex ignored GMENAC's recommendations.

When Congress exempted both the DME and the IME components of Medicare—the funds directed to teaching hospitals—from
DRGs in 1983, it also set an 11.59 percent add-on (which in the
intervening years has dropped to the current 7.7 percent) to each
DRG payment (currently at 7.7 percent) for the higher patient care
costs that teaching hospitals experience. Approximately 1,300 hospitals have one or more residency programs. Puzzling at best is the
fact that these programs have never been audited for IME. As a
result (and because academic medical centers do not have a real system of cost accounting), no one knows the true costs of GME
financing.

By 1991, GME financing from all sources had grown to approximately $14 billion. The average yearly cost of educating a resident
was estimated at $179,000 (Alliance for Health Reform, 1994); in
other words, the total revenue from GME funding to residents,
teaching physician staff, and hospital administrative and support
staff was $14 billion.

Forces Shaping Current Financing Systems

How did this process of social engineering occur—a process in
which the United States would shift from a combined primary and
specialty care–based system to an excessively specialty care–based
system? Several factors are evident. Through the process of scientific discovery and the development of medical technology, the field
of medicine became more specialized from the period just after
World War II to the present. The federal National Institutes of
Health, active in that discovery and development, were oriented to
specific diseases, such as stroke and cancer; there was no National
Institute of Primary Care. The NIH provided training through
grants, fellowships, and career development awards to both Ph.D.
and M.D. specialists. Likewise, the prestige of the Mary Lasker
Award, the Nobel Prize, and other similar forms of recognition were
attached to specialists rather than to primary care practitioners.

The fee-for-service system of the Blue Cross and Blue Shield
insurance companies—the system adopted by Medicare in the late

1960s—was an open mechanism to pay for the increasing number of procedures evolving around specialty care. Throughout the 1970s and 1980s, the insurance reimbursement system, public and private, promoted the growth of specialists' income at a rate of 2.5 times the rate of generalists' income (Boex, 1993). As a result, significant economic reward was related to being a specialist. Prior to 1993, it was possible for physicians doing a residency in their specialty to earn one-third to one-half the income of full-time practicing family practitioners in most areas of the country.

Given social recognition and monetary rewards, is it any wonder that undergraduate physicians gravitated in droves to specialties? Or that academic and hospital leaders were blinded by a runaway reimbursement system that supported the expansion of an excessive supply of specialists? After all, health insurance payments were paying both for the teaching infrastructure and for the surplus of specialists once in practice.

By 1990, purchasers in the private sector were moving their insured populations to managed-care organizations, which are generally able to extract lower fees from specialists (due to their competition for patients). By 1994, purchasers in some markets would no longer pay for teaching costs, and they expected academic teaching hospitals to become more competitive, in comparison to community hospitals, in their pricing. These purchasers of health insurance and health insurers themselves are likely to continue to negotiate for lower premiums, which will adversely affect academic health centers and teaching hospitals.

Faced with the prospect of declining revenue, academic leaders acted on two fronts:

• By the late 1980s, some astute leaders were linking the academic health centers to community-based settings, and others have more recently adopted that strategy.

In 1993, the AAMC and the United Hospital Consortium began work on a research project on the market evolution that is threatening the GME subsidies—federal budget constraints potentially limiting GME funding and government reform measures that could change the imbalance of specialists and primary care physicians. A medical education task force of deans, CEOs, and department chairpersons identified two strategic imperatives regarding medical education: (1) the need to align the clinical delivery system with the education system through the creation of additional primary care settings and the development of accountable educational partnerships with community-based settings, and (2) the need to modify the GME curriculum through radical reform and more effective education of generalist practitioners for managed-care settings.

The AAMC and the Association of Professors of Medicine have formed jointly a study group on the future of graduate medical education. That group's mission is to collect information about current initiatives to downsize and change the composition of training programs. The study group and other members of the AAMC have the opportunity to draw from the experiences of the Boston area's Community Partnership—the Center for Community Health Education, Research, and Service—which was presented at the AAMC's 1994 annual meeting in Boston, as well as from initiatives sponsored by other foundations.

• The second front has been political: to seek funds from the federal government to continue their form of social engineering. The AAMC and the Association of Academic Health Centers initially backed Senate proposals that included new trust funds totaling $70 billion in tax revenues over five years without any guarantees that the academic health centers would train the number of primary care providers needed. The proposals would subsidize the current overproduction of specialists and provide no economic incentives for the institutions to eliminate their inefficiencies as the nonteaching hospitals are doing (Kosterlitz, 1994).

In August 1994, after a negative reaction from advocates of primary care training, both associations agreed to tie the funding to some redirection toward the training of primary care providers. Concomitantly, the AAMC released its Lewin-VHI study, which states that the extra financial needs of teaching hospitals will require

$19.6 billion—$21.8 billion a year—in subsidies by the year 2000 to remain competitive with nonteaching hospitals (Dobson, Coleman, and Mechanic, 1994).

It is unlikely that Congress will pass such high subsidies. There is danger, however, that the lobbying strength of the teaching institutions—evident in the recent health reform debate on Capitol Hill—can defeat efforts for the redirection of GME to a significant primary care focus. The financial and professional interests of those institutions may impede attempts to redirect medical education programs to the new requirements, downsize the institutions that offer those programs, phase out some specialty programs, and advocate for a quantifiable set of steps to move a significant amount of program activity to ambulatory training sites.

The production factor of these teaching institutions is under fire and needs to be shifted. Some of their plants and facilities require closure or phasing out; others could be improved by moving programs out to ambulatory care settings based in the community. The old reimbursement system paid for the obsolescence and overproduction of academic health centers when they were viewed as producing revenue. Now that they are cost centers facing other cost centers—that is, community hospitals, which are prepared to compete on price and personnel—their future is questionable. Will they continue to exist; and if so, in what manner they will continue to provide services, teach, and do research?

At the moment, the Medicare GME funding continues to support an inflated training structure that produces an excess of specialists faced with diminishing job opportunities and shrinking income possibilities. That excess allows purchasers the ability to drive down payments for specialists—not a result that specialists expected when in residency training.

The Effect of Financing on Nursing

During this century, nursing has been effective in cementing its significant role in the provision of hospital-based care. Nursing schools have focused a major portion of their educational process during that period on the complex needs of the hospital patient population and on the demands of the technology available for treatment. By the mid 1980s, however, the role of nurses in hospitals had changed dramatically, due to the impact of the DRG system of payment. Hospitals served patients who were sicker, whose care was more complex, yet whose length of stay was shorter. The demands of nursing required professionals who were better trained and were prepared to supervise a variety of other types of workers. As a consequence, the better-paying administrative jobs were in hospitals, not doctors' offices or community centers. Economic rewards and prestige for nurses, like those for doctors, were hospital- rather than community-based.

Since 1980, nursing education has been changed by the development of community-based bachelor of science in nursing and primary care master's degree programs and by the rapid proliferation and expansion of associate in arts degree programs. These changes may yet prove to be beneficial in the face of managed care's emphasis on services outside hospital walls. Given their desire for lowering the cost of care, payers and purchasers of care are the current determiners of emerging systems—including the expansion of home care and extended care services, which nurses tend to direct and manage. This expansion represents employment opportunities for nurses prepared to serve in nonhospital settings and offers challenges to articulating their roles in relation to other health professionals, particularly physicians.

In some of the markets where hospitals are downsizing, both nurses and physicians find their employment opportunities in hospitals narrowing. Both professions are in need of retraining for community-based care. Both are competing—and will continue to compete—for patients. In this environment, they may come to view such competition as less than conducive to good patient services management and decide instead to team up to deliver primary care. To achieve such a redirection of the relationship between nursing and medicine, both professions will need to continue to listen to consumers, local communities, and purchasers in defining their interdisciplinary, community-based roles. That evolving definition will become the basis for the redirection of nurses, physicians, and other health professionals. Nursing educators can then find common ground with medical educators and work together to redirect the educational process.

The Impact of Managed Care

The movement to managed care requires a shift in educational programs. Rigorous and intensive teaching of office- and clinic-based community-linked methods—along with practical experience in each—will be needed.

Clinical practice guidelines being developed rapidly in managed-care organizations will become a core requirement in graduate training. Gordon Moore (1993) describes the special competencies needed at an advanced level for managed care: these competencies include "clinical prevention; understanding the health needs of populations of patients; management of health risks in work and home; clinical decision-making in managed care, including the processes and ethics involved in resource allocation; effective communication with patients and panels of patients; the doctor's role in continuous improvement in the quality of care; professional satisfaction as an employee; teamwork and practice leadership; and practice management" (p. iii). Most of these are skills consistent with those being developed in multiprofessional community-based settings in several of the Kellogg-sponsored Community Partnerships.

The increasing demand of HMOs for primary care providers has driven up the income of family practitioners. That financial incentive, along with the excess number of specialists, may inspire many undergraduate students to turn away from potential careers in specialty-driven medicine. Already in 1993 and 1994, the percentage of graduating medical students interested in pursuing generalist careers has increased. As these changes in the marketplace increasingly draw health professionals to primary care, students will expect high-caliber training sites where primary care is delivered. Consortia of community-based providers, HMOs, medical schools, and teaching hospitals can seize the opportunity to redirect GME in order to financially support community-based training sites. These sites include community health centers, clinics, doctors' offices, and schools. HMOs and the contracting partners can become the teaching settings for the retraining of faculty.

The Need to Redirect GME

Financial arrangements for teaching sites in ambulatory care settings are nonexistent—hence the demand for a redirection of GME financing. With declining patient care reimbursement derived from Medicare and insurance, teaching hospitals will find it difficult, perhaps Herculean, to transfer some of that reimbursement from their hospital department to ambulatory care sites.

The literature on practice costs shows that, for similar cases, generalists both provide a higher quality of primary care than specialists and practice a less resource-intensive style of patient care, with significant cost implications (Boex, 1993).

For almost fifty years, as we have seen, the U.S. health system has been specialty-driven. Because the public has been willing to pay more for specialist care, policy makers in government, in the private insurance sector, and in academic health centers and specialty organizations worked too successfully, one could argue, to produce and reward specialists. During the past half-century, a complex organization, an expensive infrastructure, and a maze of funding paths developed. Academic leaders adroitly modified their organizations to provide excellent teaching, research, and services. It is not surprising, therefore, that the development of a new primary care educational structure in communities will require time, imagination, and fiscal support (including a significant redirection of the current funding of health professions education).

In this debtor nation, redirection of existing funds will be easier than seeking additional dollars from government. At a time when the government has proven itself capable of closing excess military bases in the aftermath of the Cold War and of questioning even farm subsidies, elected officials will be reluctant to explain to the American public (along with business and labor interests and the press) a graduate medical education apparatus that would continue to produce surplus specialists rather than primary care providers. Primary care providers remain in short supply in many areas of the country, yet they help to make the health care system economically efficient and affordable to a broader consumer base. Policy makers pause more than briefly when they learn the following: modeling indicates that if the ratio of generalists and specialists in 1992's health care delivery system had been 50:50 rather than the actual 30:70, the projected savings would have reached $160 billion (Boex, 1993).

The sustainability and further development of a primary care training structure in communities requires the redirection of GME financing not only toward the training of generalist physicians and advanced-practice nurses committed to becoming primary care providers but also toward other health professionals trained in the multiprofessional arrangements that the Kellogg Foundation has encouraged and that managed-care organizations require. When social workers, public health professionals, dental professionals, and physician assistants engage in primary care teams and settings, GME financing should cover their training costs. As a basis for any health profession's inclusion in GME financing, economical and efficient contribution to the delivery of primary care services, including effective preventive care, should be required, and research should be ongoing to prove the level of the economic and health contribution.

There is a growing match between what the Community Partnerships model has encouraged and what academic health centers, foundations, national organizations, federal and state public policy, and market forces are ready for.

Academic health centers and their faculties in health sciences—those who have directly and indirectly enjoyed the recent largesse of a reimbursement system—are now undergoing shrinkage. They require information on how to position themselves and redirect a portion of the teaching and research focus to community-based care. Although academic institutions are inherently slow to change and academics are reluctant to revise a hospital-based curriculum that has worked well for so long, it is essential that academics in the health sciences understand and support current attempts at health care reform; only if they do can they remain both relevant to their students' occupational requirements and economically viable. It is no longer dangerously radical (if it ever was) to move a significant portion of the curriculum out of the university or hospital into the community.

The Kellogg Foundation has not been alone in the development of a knowledge base to support community-based education. Other foundations, such as The Robert Wood Johnson Foundation, The Pew Charitable Trusts, the Kaiser Family Foundation, and the Josiah Macy, Jr., Foundation have all contributed to heightened awareness of the need for a shift to the paradigm of primary care. The Pew Commission on Health Professions Education, for example, called attention (through two widely disseminated reports focused on the content of health professions education) to many of the issues addressed in the Community Partnerships initiative. In this process of research and education, foundations have highlighted the issues for those who pay for health care and health care education—showing how the payment systems have led to the overproduction of specialists and how those payments can be redirected economically to an efficient system that is based on primary care, located in the community, and complemented, not dominated, by specialty care.

Federal and state policy makers have attended to this issue as well. A perspective favoring increased access to health care through physician workforce reform is shared by the federal Council on Graduate Medical Education (COGME).

James Boex and others (1993) have documented three essential and replicable ways in which many medical schools and residency programs could increase the number of their graduates choosing community-based primary care careers: "Selection of students likely to choose such practices, implementation of primary care–based curricula including exposure to positive primary care role models, and the settings of such curricula to the largest extent possible outside of the traditional academic medical center and in the community which is to serve as the practitioner's workplace are all necessary to influence student career choice toward community-based primary care careers" (p. 11). The Community Partnerships have structured themselves to select students likely to pursue primary care careers and to educate them in curricula that are based in communities.

The shift to a primary care–driven training system has commenced at the state level—an important development, since states have a significant role in financing health professions education—and participating states can be both models and laboratories of change. During the five years from 1989 to 1994, several states developed workforce policies that provide educational support and financial incentives to medical professionals who choose training in primary care, especially in underserved areas, and opt to be trained in communities. Often these policies involve cooperative interactions between the states and local communities. Texas has targets for the percentage of medical students it wants to graduate in primary care and family practice, for example. New York weights graduate medical education funding to favor primary care. Alabama provides stipends and living expenses to students and residents to be trained in underserved communities.

A number of states have implemented scholarship and loan programs for a range of primary care practitioners and have initiated and expanded area health education centers to promote collaborative training programs by health professional schools and communities in underserved areas (Henderson, 1994).

Despite the fact that budgetary barriers have delayed development in a number of states, the states seem relatively more focused on the production of primary care providers in local communities with the dollars available to them for health professions education than does the federal government. The federal government can learn much from the states' experience and should not hinder their efforts.

Strategies for Sustaining Change

In this climate of forces congealing to support more suitably prepared primary care practitioners, any effort at redirecting health professions education toward community-based training must look to long-term financial sustainability. Multiple strategies to achieve sustainability—reallocating existing resources, securing new state and local funding, and seeking changes in GME financing that would benefit primary care training—are available. Although these are most effective used in concert, let us look at each in turn.

Reallocation of Resources

Four of the Community Partnerships have targeted reallocation of resources to sustain and expand the changes they have accomplished over the long term. Although the extent of efforts varies across the Partnerships, policy statements include such action proposals as these: requiring medical schools receiving state support to recruit and preferentially admit students likely to enter primary care specialties (especially those interested in practice in underserved areas) and to ensure that at least 50 percent of their graduates enter primary care specialties; increasing support for family practice residency programs as well as for nurse practitioner, certified nurse midwife, primary care physician assistant, and social work programs; expanding health professions scholarships and loan repayment programs targeted to primary care specialties in medically underserved areas of the state; and providing support to increase the number of community health centers.

In some of the Community Partnerships employing these strategies, project leaders have testified at the state level on related policy issues. Partnerships are actively involved in informing legislators about the need to support reallocation of funds consistent with project objectives.

Acquisition of New Funds from State and Local Sources

Two of the Partnerships seeking reallocation of resources are also involved in identifying new funding sources at either the state or local level. One additional Partnership has identified this as its primary strategy for sustainability. A fourth Partnership is seeking new funds at the state and local levels while exploring the long-term feasibility of redirecting GME funding.

In one Partnership's state, funding has been targeted over a five-year period to prepare faculty for teaching in rural communities and to provide health care services and student training in these settings. In this instance, allocation and levels of new state funding are tied to the state's need for rural health services. In another state, a loan repayment program has been designed for legislative consideration. Under the terms of this recommendation, loans would be made available to third- and fourth-year medical students, advanced-practice nursing students, and physician assistant students on the condition that they practice primary care within the state.

Partnerships have also secured new local funds—support from local foundations, for example—to expand project capabilities and services.

Changes in GME Funding

Only two of the Community Partnerships have focused on seeking changes in the system of GME financing of health professions education. In both cases, the Partnerships are in areas whose federal legislative representatives are active in health reform issues. Partnership leadership in both instances has targeted informing these influential individuals about the role that workforce policy and funding play in health care cost and access issues. Project directors at these sites provide technical assistance to legislators on workforce issues and work continually to educate policy makers, business leaders, and consumer groups on the effect of health professions workforce funding and policy.

Lessons Learned

Just as methods of financing health professions education have shaped its development, reform of health professions education may redirect financing. In the process of seeking to accomplish change in both areas, the Community Partnerships have collectively and individually identified several issues affecting progress toward change:

- Because it is extremely difficult to change academic institutions, financial leverage in the form of funding from private foundations or from the state is essential. However, funding coming from outside the university must focus on institutionalization of community-based, multiprofessional primary care training and must be perceived as contract money to the university and local communities to achieve change (rather than as special-project funds). Even with that leverage, both the magnitude and the complexity of the effort to achieve Partnership sustainability are daunting.
- In the early stages of the change process, there is a tendency to underestimate the costs of decentralizing an educational effort and relocating it within the community. A more accurate picture of the costs of community-based, ambulatory education must be determined and taken into account from the beginning if we are to successfully shift health professions education to out-of-hospital settings.
- The cooperation and enthusiastic support of educational and community leaders are critical to the success of funding change. In several Partnerships, the interest of the university president or medical school dean has been crucial to the project's acceptance and

credibility. Elsewhere, community, business, and legislative leaders have galvanized support for new approaches to funding. Whatever the source of leadership, the presence of active political support is keenly felt by those addressing funding issues.

• Partnership communication efforts must focus on political players—whether institutional or legislative—and their constituencies. Partnerships have worked through a variety of media to inform leaders at multiple levels about health professions education and the current funding practices that support it.

• Redirection of GME funding is critical to changing health professions education. Despite the very real successes in obtaining funding at local and state levels, the current Partnerships have a marginal base of support. Furthermore, other such partnerships may not develop without federal redirection of GME financing. Neither the current amount nor the current distribution of GME payments is appropriate for encouraging a reduction in the training of specialists and a redirection of graduate medical education toward primary care training. It is therefore crucial that government decisions about the capitation of Medicare and Medicaid take into account the funding of graduate medical education in community-based training sites.

• Managed care is an untapped source of possible funding for community-based health professions education. Although the Community Partnerships have explored three viable sources of financing for their academic community health systems, a very healthy and growing fourth source has been largely ignored. Given the shared interest in changing the location and relevance of health professions education today, those interested in changing that education would do well to consider managed-care organizations as a possible source of long-term funding.

• Community teaching sites do not conform to the accreditation methods used to evaluate hospital-based programs. At this point, too little is known about how to evaluate quality in community-based health professions education. Such ignorance may impair the growth and acceptance of community-based training. Accreditation methods specific to community teaching sites must be developed and phased in quickly to support the pace of reform.

These action steps can stimulate the formation of consortia to promote the development of community training programs. The difficulties of retrofitting the current teaching structure will be as painful as what the military-industrial complex has experienced. At the same time, there will be numerous opportunities to create new, more effective primary care educational programs, services, and research—and, it is hoped, a healthier population. Redirecting our financing processes is the first major challenge to overcome if we are to get an educational and service system focused on primary care.

9

Evaluation as a Tool for Reform

Rebecca C. Henry

The evaluator's role is often viewed as one of independent judge. In the early stages of a project, program leaders generally meet with evaluators to discuss the role of evaluation and to clarify audience, methods, and reporting procedures. The discussion typically involves identifying not only the desired outcomes and methods of measurement but the steps evaluators will take to prevent evaluation from influencing the program and program participants' perceptions. In general, program personnel and evaluators have very different—and distinctly separate—contributions to make to a developing program. Administrators are responsible for designing and implementing change; evaluators tell them if their efforts are successful.

Community Partnerships evaluators and program leaders interact very differently from this norm. Evaluators frequently shape meeting agendas, participate in discussions on strategic planning, and speak on behalf of the Community Partnerships initiative. Partnership program planners are likewise involved in developing evaluation instruments and interpreting data for preliminary reports. Concerns that an evaluation team's commitment to the goals of the initiative might translate into bias seem to have been set aside.

The Community Partnerships initiative has had the benefit of two kinds of evaluation: cluster evaluation and project-level evaluation. Cluster evaluation tracks the progress of the Partnerships collectively and measures their gains against the intent of the Kellogg initiative. A team of evaluators keeps in close contact with the projects by making regular visits, interviewing participants, attending meetings and activities, reviewing materials developed for the projects, and collecting data in other ways. Project-level evaluation, on the other hand, works within the goals and framework of a specific project: using many of the methods employed in cluster evaluation, each project evaluates the effectiveness and impact of the changes initiated by the Partnership's efforts. Through cluster and project-level evaluation, the Community Partnerships initiative suggests a new role for evaluation in the process of change.

While much of what we talk about as educational reform is really tinkering in the margins of one of society's oldest institutions (the university), the Community Partnerships initiative forces academe to examine its processes and products in new ways. When change cuts as deep and wide as this effort does, traditional notions of evaluation become less relevant and useful.

Many believe that if reform is accomplished, evaluation to prove its success will not be needed. There is probably some truth in that view: if one has to search too far for meaningful indicators of change, the change probably was not very significant. As the Community Partnerships have shown, one of the most interesting roles for evaluation is not in selecting the outcomes to measure but in working with the leaders of change. In this respect, the goal of evaluation is to provide data to decision makers, planners, and leaders of change to assist them in shaping reform and strengthening the strategies to accomplish it. The role of evaluation in this type of change effort is to increase the likelihood that significant and sustainable change will occur.

Participating in the change process on any level presents a significant dilemma to many evaluators and leaders of change. Those involved in the Community Partnerships are no exception. Evaluators have been socialized to value objectivity, independence, and "hard" data. But Community Partnerships evaluators need to believe in the Partnerships, to become sympathetic to the leaders and the challenges that face them, and to be willing to participate in the problem solving required by those challenges. At times, the recommendations of these evaluators have been made based on data that were incomplete and frequently "soft," though very compelling. In the Community Partnerships setting, evaluators have not had the luxury of watching from the sidelines.

Moving Beyond Traditional Evaluation Approaches

Perhaps the most common perception of an evaluator is that of an independent professional using quasi-experimental methods to determine if a program has accomplished a set of preestablished goals. Because of their close link with academic institutions, both institutional leaders and evaluators are socialized to place a heavy emphasis on empirical evidence, the scientific method, and the pursuit of truths as a primary end point. This approach is ideal when a client needs to know if a particular program has achieved outcomes that cannot otherwise be explained. When reform is the endpoint, however, neither this approach nor the traditional client-evaluator relationship is likely to be as productive.

In the case of the Community Partnerships initiative, evaluation is not equated with science, and the relationship between evaluator and reform leader is not as clear-cut as in the traditional evaluation model. In order for evaluation to facilitate reform, leaders and evaluators must step outside of traditional roles to discover new ways in which information can be used to enhance the change process.

The Community Partnerships initiative is a complex reform process bringing together academics, community leaders, and health care providers to accomplish system change. However worthy the goal of systems change, however, when the stakes are high and individual reputations are on the line, evaluation is seldom a welcome participant in the process. Some view the role of evaluation with skepticism; others see it as an outright threat. Prior experience with evaluation biases many to believe that whatever evaluation reveals will not be "good."

While there is no single dominant model of program evaluation, there has long been a struggle between those who imagine evaluation draped in the prestige of research and causal inference and those who preach that the experimental research paradigm is catastrophically inappropriate for the uncontrollable political social realities of practical program implementation (Shaddish, Cook, and Leviton, 1991).

Although some components of the Community Partnerships initiative evaluation have incorporated very traditional methods, the role that cluster and project evaluators have played in monitoring and shaping the change process would not be encouraged by some authorities in evaluation circles. Despite the evaluators' nontraditional approach, however, the evaluation efforts have had a powerful impact on the success of this initiative and are worth the consideration of other change leaders.

In the Community Partnerships initiative, evaluation tasks often involve challenging program assumptions or providing information that refines how the program is conducted. Likewise, institutional leaders play an active role in shaping the evaluation focus and interpreting the findings as they emerge. To facilitate this collaboration, evaluators attend nearly all program meetings, and program directors participate in evaluation meetings. Complex systems change, whether at the curriculum or the institutional level, means moving beyond traditional roles and processes. Using evaluation to facilitate change rather than to judge its outcome has been both challenging and helpful in accomplishing our goals.

The original plan for evaluation of the Community Partnerships initiative anticipated a rather traditional design. Because the change process demanded candid, frequent information, however, an expanded role for evaluation emerged—a role that moved evaluation closer to the programming and decision-making functions.

In the process of refining the role of evaluation, participants focused on the broad goals of the Community Partnerships initiative. The aim of the Partnerships is systems change at multiple levels: curriculum, health professions institutional policy, and public policy (local, state, federal). Simply explicating desired outcomes for each goal, as traditional evaluation methods dictate, would be insufficient. Partnership evaluators need to work with reform leaders—to understand their strategies and determine how to monitor the process to give them useful information as it develops. By working together, Community Partnership evaluators and change leaders have developed the necessary trust to exploit negative findings to achieve positive outcomes.

In this expanded role, evaluation encompasses three important, but nontraditional, functions: informing the various players, challenging program assumptions, and keeping the change agenda alive.

Informing the Players

In the midst of change, it is often exceedingly difficult to assess program impact on an institution and its participants. Change leaders are so consumed by implementation that they often overlook intermediate impact, especially during the early phases of a new program. By monitoring implementation and interacting with individuals in the field, evaluators provide program leaders with information that they would otherwise not be able to gather. In the experience of the Community Partnerships, evaluation observations often complemented the observations of program leaders and others central to the Partnerships. However, when evaluators provided a different perspective, their observations seemed to be the most useful. Such differences motivated evaluators and project leaders to think carefully about what was reported and how to interpret its impact on the change process.

An early example of this came when evaluation uncovered some resistance by Community Partnership students. Some students perceived that primary care was being "pushed" on them, although formal data collection efforts indicated strong support for the primary care theme across all participating schools. During a phone conversation with an evaluator, one program director made a passing comment about resistance at his institution. Members of the evaluation team checked this out at other sites and discovered that it was not an isolated event. Collectively, cluster evaluators discussed the issue with the initiative's leadership and strategized appropriate responses for the sites. By responding early to the students' concerns, the Partnerships were able to avoid serious problems and make useful modifications to the program.

Challenging Program Assumptions

One of the best contributions evaluation has made to the Community Partnerships initiative is its function as an occasional inside critic. By challenging the assumptions that guide the change process and considering closely the specifics of program implementation, evaluation has helped to strengthen the overall program. Evaluators need to understand the intent of a program, its philosophical underpinnings, and the logistics of implementation. By listening and learning from program leaders and asking probing questions— Why does this step need to happen this way? Wouldn't the program be just as successful without that particular requirement?—evaluators help leadership isolate the real essentials of change. Despite the fact that the Community Partnerships initiative was reviewed and shared with many informed individuals prior to implementation, for example, the plan was still imperfect and at times unrealistically complex. Listening and reacting as project leaders described the program and its implementation process, evaluators helped program leaders refine and clarify program elements.

Keeping the Change Agenda Alive

In the change process, program leaders often find themselves battling inertia. Inertia sets in if change takes too long or uncovers too many enemies. In combating inaction and resistance to change in the Community Partnerships, evaluators and program leaders came to realize the importance of real-life stories illustrating the positive impact of the change in progress. Evaluation is in a unique position to assist the forces of change in this respect. Evaluators observe, interview, witness, and participate. They see firsthand the positive effects of a developing program. They hear the stories and see the change in faculty, students, and community people. To keep participants enthusiastic and focused as the projects developed, evaluators would sometimes bring dramatic stories to light—sharing observations and incidents as well as the statistical information they had gathered. For some project participants, the impact and urgency of a single pivotal incident provided much more compelling support for the project than all the aggregated data a program collected. This "head and heart" approach to sharing the fruits of evaluation can keep the change agenda alive among project leaders and participants.

Positioning Evaluation as a Tool for Reform

One especially interesting aspect of this large initiative has been the way in which evaluation functions *within* each of the seven Community Partnerships. Each of the Partnerships operates within a unique context, with its own set of assumptions, players, institutional histories, missions, and expectations for change outcomes.

Across the Partnerships, cluster evaluators have observed two distinct ways in which project-level evaluation is conducted: "internal" and "external." While no project within the Community Partnerships initiative has an exclusively internal or external approach to evaluation, each project's efforts do seem to cluster around one or the other. Neither approach is the right or wrong way in general terms; rather, individual Partnerships need to create evaluation that responds to the needs and values of a particular program. By examining the two different models of project-level evaluation, we can identify the most effective mode of conducting evaluation at any given site.

Internal evaluation works closely with decision makers to craft a strategy that will inform the progress of the project as well as monitor its development. Internal evaluators frequently attend meetings with decision makers, contributing to the discussion and helping to set the agenda. These individuals see themselves as part of a larger management team responsible to the Partnership board for the direction and operations of the project.

Evaluators who take the internal approach are often Partnership employees; like the executive director, they are part of the project staff. Their interest in the success of the overall project is tangible, and their efforts are geared toward supporting success through thorough, candid evaluation of the design and implementation of the model. They consider the processes and outcomes of project activities as well as side effects and unintended consequences. These evaluators report to both staff and board decision makers frequently. The contact with the executive director, in fact, is often quite informal. In two Partnerships, the offices of the evaluator and the program director are so close to each other that one would expect interaction on a daily basis.

Internal evaluators are frequently called upon to perform tasks well outside the domain of traditional evaluation. Their roles are ambiguous and ever-changing. While this "stretch" sometimes causes discomfort for evaluators, the nontraditional tasks do bring them closer to the inner workings of the program and enhance their ability to connect evaluation to the overall success of the project.

External evaluation is more likely to have the evaluator functioning independent of the program director and core leadership team. External evaluators collect data and report to project leadership, but they do it formally and at less frequent intervals. Their data collection focuses on process and outcomes exclusively. Their more traditional role is to use the findings to objectively assess the success of the project.

Evaluators employing the external approach are often "on loan" from a Partnership institution. They work with the project director in a supervisor-subordinate relationship. Although their role in project operations is narrower than that of internal evaluators, it is one that is clearly defined and familiar to most evaluators.

It should also be noted that each of these approaches has both strengths and weaknesses. For example, internal evaluators are positioned to have a good understanding of their project, and they have access to many important discussions that influence the direction evaluation can take. On the other hand, these individuals have been known to be overwhelmed by the range of demands placed on them by their program leaders. Because they are so knowledgeable about the program, they are called upon to function in a variety of roles. External evaluators, on the other hand, have the security of an approved evaluation plan, but they miss opportunities to modify it based upon inside information.

When it comes to reform, it seems that evaluation can best serve leadership when it positions itself very close to decision making and decision makers. There are obvious risks to this approach—especially when the approach is judged by traditionalists, who are accustomed to evaluation that functions as an applied experiment. But because system reform is fluid and unpredictable, evaluations that rely exclusively on preset outcomes run the risk of being irrelevant to the change process. Evaluation that works closely with leadership, on the other hand, is in less danger of "missing" the change. Such an evaluation method evolves *with* the project rather than in the wake of it.

Lessons in Evaluation

The following eight evaluation "lessons," drawn from the experience of the Community Partnerships, may be instructive to educational leaders and evaluators contemplating a new type of interaction:

• *Change is not empirically driven.* Those in academe sometimes trust data too much. A common misconception is that if the data demonstrate that meaningful measurable outcomes are achieved, the reform can be considered a success. Essentially, change is a political and institutional process, however, and evaluators need to understand it as such. Most significant change occurs in a data vacuum and is driven by carefully crafted messages, stories, and a sufficient amount of evidence for the influential opinion leaders to be convinced of its importance. As comfortable as evaluators and program leaders are with hard data, change is the product of a variety of forces, many of them quite "soft."

• *Incomplete data now are worth more than complete data later.* Evaluators are not comfortable with their data being used prematurely. To avoid this, they often overanalyze, reanalyze, and interpret until there are so many restrictions that the data are essentially useless to the consumers of the report. Decision makers cannot wait for the perfect data set: evaluators who seek to provide it may be left behind as program leaders move on to the next issue. Timing is everything.

• *Anticipate the nay-sayers.* Any evaluation textbook advises evaluators to identify and understand different audiences. This is especially important when evaluators are working in reform. Too often evaluators preach to the converted, sadly missing opportunities to interact and communicate with those influentials who can impede the change process. By understanding various audiences' concerns with the proposed reform, the evaluator can select targeted outcomes and process markers that address those concerns and deliver the needed findings at timely intervals. For example, policy makers at the local, state, and national level are a crucial audience for long-term sustainability of the Community Partnerships. A great deal of effort at the project level has therefore been directed at informing these groups about the cost of education and at providing local community stories, adding a human element to the need for the reform.

• *Don't shoot the evaluator.* If evaluation is to play a meaningful role in reform, there must be ample opportunity for evaluators and leaders to share information openly and honestly without the fear of negative consequences. In searching to identify the positive impact of reform, evaluators frequently miss important findings that tell us that the program or process is not working according to plan. Successful Partnership leaders are skillful at using unexpected and undesirable observations to strengthen the quality of the reform effort.

• *Objective data can lie*. Objective is "good" and subjective is "bad," right? Not always. Objective data have a place in evaluation, but they should be complemented with subjective findings for balance. In preintervention surveys with Community Partnerships faculty and students, for instance, evaluators uncovered very strong and positive beliefs about the importance of multidisciplinary learning and practice. Unfortunately, out in the field, a major impediment to progress has been the inability of the different professionals to put turf battles behind them. The subjective findings have proved much more useful for instituting planning changes than the more formalized, systematic data collections.

• *Evaluation is too important to be given away to evaluators*. Program leaders need to participate in the evaluation process. In order to have a sense of the climate for change and to understand the impact the reform is making, leaders need to collect some of the data firsthand. Leaders need to leave the conference rooms and talk to individuals who are affected by the change. Despite the fact that the leaders of the Community Partnerships reform effort are seasoned institutional figures, they have had several key lessons to be learned about community, academic institutions, and how they interact. Changes have had to be made in the programming goals to accommodate the real world. Leaders open to learning by participating in evaluation techniques have been able to make changes to strengthen the long-term viability of the initiative.

• *Attend to the message*. While evaluation data can play an important part in the change process, the message that packages and delivers the data can be even more important. The Community

Partnerships have certainly had no dearth of data describing the processes and products of the program. What was missing initially was a vehicle to get that work to key audiences. For example, although most evaluators and Partnership spokespeople have strong links to academe, many of the Partnerships' target audiences—especially those in the policy arena—do not share this background. Those Partnership evaluators who have crafted their most important messages and results for academic audiences have found that public decision makers—the ones who *need* to know about the partnerships—have not always been receptive to their findings. Scholarly communication, then, is inadequate for many purposes. Collectively, the Community Partnerships have learned that matching the message to the audience is essential.

- *Don't be afraid to draw the finish line on the reform process.* One major question that needs to be addressed is, When does the reform process end, meaning that victory (or defeat) can be declared? As is obvious to anyone who has been centrally involved in institutional change, a meaningful end point is difficult to define. From the leader's position, an early declaration is usually advantageous, because most institutions cannot sustain a protracted change process without new and often unforeseen barriers cropping up. From the evaluator's position, there are always interesting outcome and process data to be collected—data that provide deeper understanding of the ultimate impact of the reform. Despite these different orientations, it is often necessary and appropriate to "write the last chapter." Although evaluators resist it, reform often demands it.

In the Community Partnerships initiative, the "last chapter" may not occur for four or five more years. During this time frame, students' long-term career decisions will be made. The challenge to evaluators will be to reveal important preliminary findings that are suggestive of outcomes without waiting until the actual outcomes can be measured. As with other reform processes, when the final outcome data emerge from this program, most leaders will be on to new domains of interest.

This chapter has described an alternative look at program evaluation—one that serves as a tool for the reform process rather than as a means for judging its success. This approach is no panacea. It requires all partners—program personnel and evaluators alike—to step out of traditional roles and move beyond existing perceptions to see what evaluation can accomplish. Most program leaders are not inclined to use evaluation to promote change; rather, they use it to prove the efficacy of change after the fact. But leaders of reform need assistance from all fronts if reform is to be successful. Work with the Community Partnerships initiative suggests that a close linkage between evaluators and reform leadership can yield very positive results and shape reform efforts in the process.

10

Multidisciplinary Care and Education

Patricia T. Castiglia

An underlying premise of the Community Partnerships initiative is that changes must be made in the current health care system to make it more accessible and cost-effective. Yet in order for change to occur in health care, the attitudes and practices of health care providers must change. This problem is one that could be addressed in terms of either the existing workforce or the future workforce. The Community Partnerships initiative has taken the latter route, believing that by focusing on health professions students, reformers can implement change in a more determined and effective manner. Students early in their careers have not yet been indoctrinated into the established boundaries of each profession and can therefore be influenced in the way they will practice.

In the existing health care system, physicians are the major decision makers. They decide the direction of care. In truth, however, doctors cannot provide comprehensive care alone. Their education focuses on a medical model that is essentially illness-oriented. Even in community sites, physicians are generally focused on the patient's illness, not on maintaining his or her health. Educational experiences, time limitations, and health care reimbursement policies all shape physicians' practice habits, of course. Yet when physicians speak of primary care, they are generally speaking of the first encounter with a patient—one prompted by the individual's need for medical care.

Even if comprehensive care could be given by physicians alone, it would be much too costly given our current reimbursement system. And with so many qualified health professionals available to bring their distinct skills and perspectives to a patient's care, it would be a waste of expertise to confine patient care to physician-only care.

The Multidisciplinary Approach

Multidisciplinary care shifts the emphasis from the episodic relationship between patient and physician to care from a variety of different professionals working in a system coordinated around patient needs. The shift is from a traditional, illness-based approach to a community health approach in which care is population-based as well as patient-based. Rather than seeing the patient apart from his or her environment, care in this model places the patient within the context of community to ensure that all aspects of health are considered in treatment.

Multidisciplinary care also takes the view that many qualified health professionals contribute to the comprehensive care of a patient. Nurses, social workers, dentists, public health workers—all these have much to offer comprehensive patient care. Just as the perspective, knowledge base, and skills of each profession are different, each profession's role in patient care is distinct as well. Multidisciplinary care embraces the individual professions and their roles and responsibilities, but it seeks to link them into a system focused on patient needs. A multidisciplinary system takes advantage of the capabilities of many health professionals to deliver comprehensive patient care.

Although the idea of multidisciplinary care may not be new, multidisciplinary education of health professionals is still considered somewhat risky for many professional schools. The Community Partnerships initiative's inclusion of multidisciplinary education as part of the model was intended to address this reticence on the part of academic institutions. The Community Partnerships approach suggests that by creating multidisciplinary systems of care in communities and putting students in them for a significant portion of their training, health professions education institutions and their partners can offer students new, cooperative ways of practicing their respective disciplines. In these multidisciplinary systems, Partnership students from the various health professions often learn together—participating in shared clinical experiences, jointly problem-solving "best" approaches, and collaborating on case management.

The Partnerships' focus on multidisciplinary education through multidisciplinary care assumes that this approach will have a number of long-term benefits. One is an improvement in the quality of care. When doctors, nurses, and other health professionals work together to care for patients, the care they deliver is likely to be more comprehensive. Another benefit may be cost reduction: a multidisciplinary care system that appropriately utilizes the skills of many different health professionals has the potential to reduce duplication of services, fragmentation of care, and cumbersome administration. A third expected benefit rests with the quality of education that health professions students stand to receive in community-based multidisciplinary care settings. Students educated in this way will know firsthand both the challenges and benefits of multidisciplinary care. Whatever their discipline, they will be better able to function in managed-care organizations and other settings looking to develop viable multidisciplinary patient care systems.

Despite these looked-for enhancements to health care and health professions education, multidisciplinary education is not without its barriers. In the course of the Community Partnerships' work, all seven projects have contributed to understanding both the barriers and the benefits of multidisciplinary education.

Barriers to Multidisciplinary Education

Negative attitudes toward multidisciplinary education are expressed in a variety of forms. Why tamper with a good thing? some would say. It is a great deal of work to change curriculum and training, others point out. What if the effort is not successful? Change may be too risky, some voices suggest. What if pass rates on licensing and certifying examinations fall? Students might not like the new curriculum, while faculty might resent additional time demands for planning, implementing, and evaluating the new curriculum. The reasons go on and on.

Many of the concerns voiced by those supporting the status quo raise important issues. The barriers to achieving multidisciplinary education are very real, and they are present both within academic institutions and outside them. Only by recognizing the barriers and anticipating the difficulties can those who support multidisciplinary education lay the groundwork for lasting change.

Issues for Academic Institutions

Control issues almost always emerge around curriculum change. This is especially true when reformers are designing multidisciplinary educational experiences. Who "owns" certain content? Can faculty relinquish what they perceive as their discipline's approach for the common learning desired? Can diverse faculty members supervise and teach students from a variety of disciplines? Filibustering is used in curriculum discussions as effectively as in politics: stalling the solution of issues may result in abandonment or at least cause serious delay.

In academic institutions' clinical sites, programmatic issues with a control theme evolve. Who sees the most interesting patients? Who sees the paying patients? Who sets the pace for patient activity? Who dominates the conference discussions?

Less obvious control issues, too, may emerge among physicians and nurses. Language and behavior send messages. How does the "masculine" medical model affect multidisciplinary training efforts? Medical faculty members may refer to the nurse practitioners or nurse faculty as "the girls." Patients may assume that a male nurse must be a doctor or that a female doctor must be a nurse. (Sometimes no one even attempts to correct these misperceptions. Indeed, the incorrectly named professional may actually like the misnomer.) In one Partnership, a male physician faculty member, in discussing the practice site, made the statement that a female nurse faculty member was functioning under his license. When reminded that she functioned under her own license, he clarified that he meant he was the collaborating physician for the site. Although this type of gender issue is not a new difficulty in health professions training, it can present a barrier to multidisciplinary education.

Faculty rewards present another area of key concern for academe. Faculty involved in significant change efforts worry about their ability to progress in terms of promotion and tenure. When a faculty member expends a great deal of professional time developing innovative educational approaches and working on committees, there is little time left for research and publication. Faculty need to become aware that their research can be embodied in what they are doing. They need to be encouraged to collaborate with others in publishing. For some professions—such as medicine, where "bench" research has predominated—a more inclusive rather than exclusive attitude toward community health research must be fostered. What does it mean for a faculty member to be looked upon as "second-class" because he or she cannot receive NIH funding for community-based research? And why, if there is funding available for community research, is it usually much less than that afforded to more "scientific" investigations? These issues compound the difficulty of getting faculty out of academic health centers and into communities.

Another potential barrier relates to the fact that all health professions education programs are concerned with accreditation and licensing. Programs cannot exist for long if they cannot be accredited by their professional organizations and approved by their states. Students select schools that have acceptable pass rates on state board examinations (licensing). Therefore, all programmatic and faculty issues are reviewed within this context.

Student attitudes may also be a barrier. Students in various disciplines may perceive training with other students as a benefit—or they may not. The logistics of multidisciplinary training may have a bearing on their attitudes. Travel to rural areas, for example, where a number of the projects concentrate their experiences, may present a barrier to students if it is time-consuming and expensive. Inconveniences and other difficulties may color student perceptions about multidisciplinary education.

Issues Among the Professions

Most professionals believe that the core of any profession lies in the characteristic of autonomy. Autonomy defines how a professional can and should function, as prescribed by the rights and responsibilities of the profession. In the past, states William Honan (1994), scholars would transcend academic borders to borrow a particular skill from another discipline and then retreat back to their own discipline. In more recent times, he maintains, the increased interaction among disciplines is changing the disciplines themselves.

This trend is quite evident among health care professions. It has been more than twenty years since nurse practitioners appeared on the scene. They "borrowed" assessment skills and management of common illnesses from physicians. Their acquisition of these skills transformed the nature of graduate nursing completely. By the same token, medical schools have borrowed from various disciplines to refine communication, research, teaching, and evaluation knowledge and ability. Curricula of medical schools today emphasize educational objectives and evaluation plans. Accountability and cost containment have been borrowed from the business management field by all health care professions, and these terms have become part of our thinking and language.

Despite this ongoing interchange of skills and knowledge, the various health care professions still tend to guard against collaboration to preserve their autonomy. The separate funding streams for different health professions schools within a single university underscore this tendency. Within academic institutions, health professions schools tend to compete with each other for resources and prestige. Outside of educational institutions, professional organizations preserve the autonomy of differing professions. Medical societies, nursing associations, and social work groups channel specific information to their constituents, provide guidance on policy issues that affect them (funding, prescription privileges, licensure), and advocate for their members. The autonomy of doctors, nurses, social workers, and other health professionals is an important aspect of professional identity. The perception of the multidisciplinary approach as "collaborative"—even though it builds on the differences among professionals within a patient-focused system—may be a barrier to full participation by some professions.

Issues of Delivery Systems

One substantial barrier to providing multidisciplinary health professions education in out-of-hospital settings is the fact that few multidisciplinary care settings exist. Most systems for delivery of health services are based on the medical model. If we want to teach students clinical skills in multidisciplinary care settings, more often than not those settings must be created. The challenge of adapting an existing community care site to a multidisciplinary model may be a daunting one for most educators. Tackling adaptation of delivery systems means addressing the barriers among professions as well as the indifference and ignorance of consumers and policy makers.

The general public does not understand or value multidisciplinary care. People's experience with health professionals outside of doctors and nurses is limited at best. Even someone who knows the titles of different health professionals may be confused about their roles in the health care system: people in communities, decision makers in business and industry, and policy makers do not know what makes a nurse practitioner different from a physician's assistant, for example. Under the circumstances, then, proponents of multidisciplinary education may be asking community people, business leaders, and policy makers to support something they do not understand. To actively support the creation of community-based multidisciplinary care sites, these laypeople need to be educated about the roles of the various health care providers in comprehensive care and shown how a multidisciplinary approach can both increase access to care and limit cost.

Although these barriers present difficult challenges, strategies can be implemented to decrease their effect. Multidisciplinary educational models that successfully address some of these barriers have been developed in the Community Partnerships. Let us turn now to some of the characteristics shared by those models.

Characteristics of Successful Multidisciplinary Models

In the Community Partnerships model, community needs shape education. Working in community settings, students learn by what they see and do. To learn comprehensively, therefore, students must be in settings where multidisciplinary care is delivered. Sites must be established and professional faculty and community members educated, in order to implement the multidisciplinary model.

• *Team teaching and learning.* Students constitute both the product and one of the participants in the educational experience. They have a vested interest in obtaining the best education possible so that they can be competitive in the work arena. Because of that, students may question the value of a multidisciplinary educational model. They tend to focus on "what I need to know," " what gets me through licensure," and "how to conserve time for the important." If students do not see the value in multidisciplinary education, they will either not participate or participate only in a superficial manner.

Faculty-student interactions constitute the most accepted teaching-learning model. Students learn in various ways, but the Socratic method of one-on-one interaction has stood the test of time as perhaps the most effective method. In the Community Partnerships model, community members also are considered faculty. Therefore, they must learn the faculty role so that they can function as teachers.

There is a general consensus among participating health care faculty that both didactic and experiential components must be part of curriculum change. A shared didactic emphasis (interdisciplinary) means that students hear the same content, questions, and responses as they participate in classes with a variety of faculty members from a number of health care disciplines. The didactic format provides the traditional academic atmosphere, whether teaching is conducted on campus or at community sites. Formal classes or seminars give the learning situation a certain credibility through historical antecedents.

• *Commitment at multiple levels.* Of all those involved in the multidisciplinary effort, deans have been identified as the key to program success. Their commitment and influence regarding multidisciplinary education is crucial. If deans are neutral or nonsupportive, there appears to be little or no chance of success. The second most committed group essential for success is the multiprofessional curriculum committee. This committee ensures the integrity of the basic concepts of community-based education and multidisciplinary education. The curriculum committee is responsible for designing coursework, monitoring its implementation, and evaluating its effectiveness.

In some settings, this committee is involved in recruiting students for the community-based educational experience; in other projects, each discipline recruits its own students. (Although the recruiters vary from site to site, most of the projects do recruit students desiring to participate rather than assigning students to the project. This self-selection by students may contribute to success, because their interest is present as a basis for the experience.) Other people whose commitment has been identified as essential for success include the community-based faculty, the project director, project administrators, and executive directors of facilities such as community health centers.

• *Participation strategies.* Effective models also include successful strategies to achieve the goals of multidisciplinary education. All Community Partnerships projects have identified the need to develop strategies to effect changes in curricula, student and faculty attitudes, continued administrative awareness and support, practice settings, and faculty development, recognition, and rewards. Commonly employed strategies include orientation programs that emphasize not only factual but also experiential aspects. At one site, new students are oriented to the project through a community-wide effort. Students engage in scavenger hunts as a means to explore and meet members of the community. They have dinner with community members individually and in groups. At another site, students organize and implement health fairs and education projects in community centers and senior centers. Students must be made to feel that they "belong" in some sense to the community, and community members need to feel that the students are "theirs." The success of this approach is demonstrated by the deep commitment identified by both community members and students who have experienced it.

Another strategy common to all projects is multidisciplinary team teaching. All Community Partnerships projects have multidisciplinary teams educating at the sites. All have "site-based" or "field" faculty. All employ techniques such as multidisciplinary seminars, on-site conferences, and community projects (for example, community assessments). A number of projects have developed learning centers equipped with computer and other teaching/learning resources.

Site-based faculty are extremely important to the success of community-based multidisciplinary education. On-site faculty must be oriented to the philosophy, objectives, and goals to be effective. One project has a site manager—a faculty member—at each site. This person is a master's-prepared nurse practitioner. Only a portion of this complex advanced-practice role is direct service: the site manager is the administrator for all activities and coordinates and participates in educational experiences. In another project, field professors may be physicians in private practice or nurses in clinics who have been selected to serve as mentors because of their interest and enthusiasm as well as their expertise. There must be a mechanism or forum for on-site faculty to come together with campus-based faculty to share experiences and to actively participate in decisions relevant to the experience. Site-based faculty must also participate in all aspects of the evaluation process.

• *Curriculum change.* Strategies to effect curriculum change vary in complexity and are affected by a variety of factors. Institutional curriculum committees are frequently viewed as gatekeepers. Members of the curriculum committee must know the existing curriculum very well. They must know what is happening in their discipline and be aware of trends. All curriculum changes, such as added courses, amended credit allocations, and revised sequencing of courses, must be reviewed by the curriculum committee. The recommendations of the curriculum committee must then be made to the general faculty. If approved, proposed changes must proceed to the university committee responsible for such review—a body such as the university undergraduate committee or the faculty senate. In public universities, substantive changes may need to be approved at the state level. As this brief description illustrates, curriculum change can be a long process. It is essential that administrators—especially some key administrator, such as a dean—monitor the progress so that delays are minimized.

Multidisciplinary Education Approaches

Although each of the seven Community Partnerships is as unique as the community it serves and the institutions that form it, three approaches to multidisciplinary education have evolved among the Partnerships: the experiential approach, the academic approach, and the "parallel play" approach.

The *experiential approach* has been implemented in two partnerships—one urban, one rural. In this model, the multidisciplinary aspect of curriculum has focused on the student's learning experiences on-site. A great deal of site development has been done to cultivate an environment conducive to learning. While students participate in conferences and seminars together, the emphasis is on "learning by doing" together. Emphasis is placed on developing faculty role models on-site—faculty members who function in a multidisciplinary manner. Students focus on multidisciplinary case presentations and multidisciplinary community projects. The underlying premise of this approach is that barriers between the disciplines will dissipate through one-on-one encounters.

The *academic approach* is best illustrated by one of the rural partnership projects. All of the student experiences in that project occur at two academic community health centers developed to meet the needs of two rural communities. Before enrolling in the Partnership program, all students participate in a three-credit orientation course. For the next two years students participate in multidisciplinary education one day a week at various community sites (such as nursing homes, clinics, and physicians' offices). Required courses for the program—thirteen in all—are taught on-site also. All courses are experiential, community-oriented, and population-focused.

Four of the projects employ a *"parallel play" approach*. Although the students share some experiences, each discipline maintains "control" over its own students. For example, medical students are always assigned to and work under the direction of a physician preceptor; nursing students are primarily under the supervision of a nursing faculty member. A great deal of concern about "what the students need to know" permeates this model.

Lessons for Developing and Implementing Multidisciplinary Education

The Community Partnerships—collectively and individually—are covering new territory in multidisciplinary education. A great deal of work lies ahead. But the first few years of efforts have identified some valuable lessons for others seeking to modify health professions education.

• The first lesson, learned very early in the Community Partnerships process, is that talking about multidisciplinary education is easier than implementing it. Conflicts between medicine and nursing continue to resurface within each project. Putting in place mechanisms to make a curriculum change can take a long time, and eliciting support for change in policy and curriculum also takes time and effort. It takes planning for "all" faculty to belong to "all" students, and faculty need preparation to successfully model the multidisciplinary role. Scheduling a substantial number of students and faculty is difficult and may lead to problems in forming multidisciplinary teams. Although many may agree on the concept behind multidisciplinary education and the potential benefits, the practicalities of putting it into practice are very complicated.

• Another important lesson is that faculty and students must get involved with the community in a two-way effort. The educational institution needs to go to the community at a variety of times (not only when the institution wants something) and in a variety of ways. The educational institution should support the community's efforts by its presence and participation at multiple functions, keep in close contact with community representatives, have regular information-sharing meetings to raise awareness about multidisciplinary issues and to solicit support, and consider developing a newsletter or other communication channel.

As issues evolve, the educational institution should inform community representatives and encourage their voice in problem solving. Community members' straightforward approaches to turf battles and other difficulties among professions may be surprisingly effective. Community members are interested and want to participate in the educational process. They assist by bringing community resources to the educational milieu and functioning as teachers. They are effective because they take this role seriously. Community support and involvement should thus be sought throughout the development and implementation of multidisciplinary education.

• All state university systems are undergoing fiscal analysis, and many are involved in retrenchment. Pressure to generate external funding for educational institutions may diminish multidisciplinary efforts if universities are pressured to produce research and service dollars. Direct patient care, rather than effective teaching models, is the focus of current health care reform. Given the much-needed emphasis on service considerations, how can teaching money for all disciplines be allocated to universities to support multidisciplinary teaching models?

It is absolutely essential that a commitment be made by administrators, faculty, students, and community members to the multidisciplinary, community-based educational model. This is achieved primarily through dialogue—both one-on-one and in small-group exchanges. Meetings must be held on a regular basis to maintain the momentum, and off-campus faculty must be included in discussion sessions so that they play an active role in the educational process.

Admission, promotion, and tenure committees must be informed about the demands and significance of multidisciplinary education. They must be prepared to look at existing criteria and to consider what are reasonable expectations for faculty so involved. Faculty must be encouraged to publish articles in refereed journals on the work and research they are doing. The basic standards for promotion and tenure may not change with a shift to a multidisciplinary focus, but weightings for research, publication, teaching, and service may.

• To support multidisciplinary education, institutions can form internal organizational structures compatible with the desired changes. Few academic institutions have an organizational structure that supports multidisciplinary education as a concept—in spite of the fact that, within medical schools for example, departments of obstetrics and gynecology, internal medicine, family medicine, and pediatrics identify most of their clinical objectives to be the same. On the contrary, institutions tend to allow health professions schools and departments to function with relative autonomy. Without an internal organizational structure to link related departments and schools, multidisciplinary education will remain the exception rather than the norm. Fostering the development of internal organizational structures to link departments and schools may provide a mechanism for multidisciplinary education to develop.

However it is configured, multidisciplinary education is in the mainstream of upcoming academic trends, and it is the bearer of many benefits to students, health professionals, and the communities they serve. Its strength lies in its ability to draw on the distinct skills and perspectives of multiple health care providers to meet patient needs. To successfully teach the next generation of health professionals how to deliver care in multidisciplinary, community-based settings, we need to create and manage them today. Although creating settings for multidisciplinary care and education is no simple task, the energy required is a worthy investment in the future of health professionals and communities.

. . . .

11

Leading Educational Reform

Ronald W. Richards

Some readers, on looking at the table of contents of this book, may have immediately skipped to this final chapter. There are several possible reasons for such an action. Everybody seems to be writing about leadership, and it would be useful to find out whether there is anything new in this chapter. Many readers are "under the gun" to achieve the reforms implied by the title of the book. Finding out how to reform effectively would take some of the pressure off. Furthermore, reading this chapter might help frame an orientation to other chapters in the book (or perhaps even make it unnecessary to read them).

For whatever reason, this chapter on leading reform may be of particular interest, especially for the academic leaders of educational reform. The crucial role of leadership in fostering the reforms described in earlier chapters—a role alluded to frequently—is now the focus. And although this final chapter is written for all readers, it may have special significance for academic leaders of educational reform. They, after all, are the people asking a key question: How do I lead educational reform?

Leadership is a very popular subject. Many books have been written about it. One of the preeminent theorists on leadership, James MacGregor Burns, concludes that "leadership is one of the most observed and least understood phenomena on earth" (1978, p. 2). Joseph Rost further states, "It should be no surprise that scholars and practitioners have not been able to clarify what leadership is, because most of what is written about leadership has to do with its peripheral elements and content rather than with the essential nature of leadership as a relationship" (1991, p. 5).

At the risk of oversimplifying, I will identify here several recurring themes in the extensive literature on leadership that relate to the type of leadership needed for educational reform. Burns, for example, says that leaders need to be moral visionaries to accomplish "transformational leadership." The transformational leader, he explains, recognizes followers' roles in the leadership process. The effective leader identifies followers' needs and seeks to motivate followers to act by satisfying their higher needs.

Participatory management has emerged in the leadership literature as a practical application of early human relations work (Etzioni, 1961; Maslow, 1954). While there are variations, most participatory management stresses building teams to create an open environment in which new ideas and learning from mistakes are valued.

Another theme in the leadership literature is the need for good leaders to know themselves. They have a solid understanding of their personal strengths, weaknesses, and motivations. They allow others to grow and become as capable as they can be—even if that means being "better" than the leader.

Much of the leadership literature is based on research about and experience in U.S. corporations. Potential leaders are thought of as corporate managers—those on the way up and those who have arrived. In the abstract, it is hard to argue with leadership guidance that urges vision, attention to followers, participation in decision making, and a full understanding of the self. But the question for those who choose (or find themselves with) the responsibility to lead change in health professions education is not so much, What do we know about leaders and leadership? but rather, How do we lead our organization to change amid so many negative forces?

The Community Partnerships initiative offers lessons about leadership for those who would undertake this type of massive system change. Examining the approach to leadership of the Community Partnerships model, and the lessons learned in implementing it, provides guidelines for others attempting to reform health professions education.

The initiative's structure and point of departure were based on three specific premises about how to lead change. First, no matter how hard you try, no matter how sure you are of the correctness of your ideas and approach, no leader can do it alone. No one leader in any academic institution—whatever the personal attributes and however influential the position—has sufficient power to initiate and accomplish extensive change single-handedly.

Second, leaders gain the power they need by giving it away—to the right people, to the right places, consistent with their vision of how things ought to be; it is only by giving power away that leaders can gather the mandate they need to lead change. Giving away power—or perhaps, more correctly, *control*—is very difficult for most leaders, however. And even leaders who are prepared to do it face the often bigger challenge of determining how to give power, to whom, and for what purpose.

Third, change in institutions usually occurs in response to outside pressures, as has been noted. Work in academic settings is often dangerously insulated from the socioeconomic and political realities of the external environment. To prompt change on the inside, leaders need to form effective coalitions with the outside—among community groups and others with a legitimate interest in the mission of the institution.

Taken together, these three premises underscore the guiding principle for leading health professions educational reform: *a leader must build coalitions and work from outside in to initiate and support lasting change*. All that has been learned from the Community Partnerships flows from this belief. The Community Partnerships address the gap between what people want from their health providers and what current educational systems deliver. The Partnerships seek to educate primary care practitioners by placing students in multidisciplinary teams in academic community health systems for significant amounts of time during their training. The organization at the center of each Partnership—the linking structure that bridges the cultures of academic health centers and communities—is essentially a formal coalition designed to lead reform from the outside in.

To initiate and lead the change that health professions education requires, leaders need to fully understand and act upon the dynamics of both academic health centers and communities, they need to build organizational structures to which communities and academic health centers can give power, and they need to attend to the public policy context in which all of this takes place.

Academic Health Centers

Academic health centers are combinations of health professions schools and one or more hospitals, all associated in one way or another with a university that grants degrees and conducts research. Like all organizations, academic health centers have a desire for self-preservation, a perception that sharing power is losing control, and a tendency to differentiate into smaller and smaller groups of expertise toward the perceived autonomous ideal for the expert faculty member. The character of academic health centers is a function of these tendencies and the funding that supports their activities.

As was elaborated in Chapter Eight, academic health centers are funded by a combination of medical research, fees for clinical services provided by faculty members, and the reimbursement of costs for treating a particular illness in hospitals. The nature of the education offered by most health professions schools is an outgrowth of the way money for care and education is targeted to hospitals. Because of that, changing the training and location of health professions education has had few allies within existing systems.

Fortunately, there are some signs that this situation is changing. But the departments and schools most likely to support a redirection of health professions education—for example, family medicine, general internal medicine, community medicine, public health, and community health nursing—have little financial or faculty reward capacity to make it happen. Their potential to effect change is further compromised by their inclination to fight each other rather than work together.

Nevertheless, understanding and acting upon the dynamics of academic health centers is pivotal in leading change in health professions education. Leaders seeking health professions educational reform should consider the following lessons relative to academic health centers when crafting a viable approach:

- *Have a vision; articulate it simply.* This often-stated lesson applies to leaders in any effort but is critical to leaders of health professions educational reform. The vision, and a clear articulation of it, draws people to the change process. There is power in the vision and conviction of a leader. That power grows when the vision and its rationale are understood and believed.

The power of a clearly articulated vision has been apparent in many of the Community Partnerships. The vision's articulation has come from communities at times, academe, and in some instances the Partnership itself. In one case, a community leader's observation—"I don't think there's anything I wouldn't do to achieve the goals of the Community Partnership"—not only expressed her conviction but consistently guided her actions. Another community leader spoke of dreams for her children and grandchildren and remarked that the Partnership students would be role models showing those she loved how education could help them.

Academic leaders have been another source of vision. One nursing dean's plain statement of fact spoke eloquently to the need to offer care beyond the convenience of regular business hours. Looking up from scrubbing walls in preparation for the opening of a new after-hours clinic, the dean remarked, "People work nine-to-five. Why not have providers available in the evening and on weekends?"

Medical leadership has been the source of vision as well. "Academic health centers," said one vice president for health affairs, "have an ethical, moral obligation to be responsive. If the system isn't right, academic health centers have an obligation to create new models. That's what we're paid by society to do!"

In still other situations, the vision has been a collective one articulated by Partnership leaders. One leader, convinced that neither nursing nor medicine alone can meet the primary care needs of people, has time and again articulated her belief that out-of-hospital, multidisciplinary models of care and education are essential to meeting the needs of people. But she has done so in a simple, compelling challenge to her peers: "If we don't do it together, who will?"

• *Link change to an institution's history and values.* An academic health center's parent university has both history and values to guide it. Land-grant universities, for example, are different historically than other types of state-supported institutions. Likewise, rural universities have a very different character than urban ones. Successful change strategies are built on such history and values and are often closely linked to the university's culture and purpose. Organizations cannot tolerate visions that are too far outside their historical character. Leaders who espouse such visions may be perceived as fanatics—too far outside the culture of the institution to lead it.

All of the Community Partnerships have academic health centers that historically have embraced research and specialty care. However, all of them also embrace a responsiveness to the primary health care needs of society. Some institutions can and should survive and thrive in the future by doing research and specialty care well. Partnership projects add to research and specialization the dimension of linking with communities to meet primary health care needs.

Some of the Partnerships are institutions based upon an agricultural tradition of helping people in rural communities statewide through Cooperative Extension Services. In these institutions, the Community Partnerships initiative is consistent with that historical intention. In urban areas, some of the Partnerships are linked to universities distinguished by a long-standing concern for giving people who would not otherwise get to college an opportunity for higher education.

Not all of the Community Partnerships are clear about their historical roots. However, it seems to be characteristic of medical schools—all graduate schools, for that matter—to want to emulate high-powered, nationally recognized research universities ("Research I's," in the vernacular of academe). In doing so, some institutions deny their historical roots. Good leaders link the intentions of educational reform to aspects of an institution's historical character and core values.

• *Know where the sharks are, who they feed with, and what they eat.* Leading educational reform requires an accurate map of an academic health center's power configuration. Sometimes mapping can be started by looking at the physical manifestations of organizational power—the amount of space a department is given, the number of NIH grants it has, its clinical income, and its full-time equivalents. Often, though, the inquiries and observations need to go deeper. Leaders need to understand clearly which departments and individuals are the most influential: Who might be allies and enemies to the proposed change, and why? What is the relationship between the academic health center and the parent university? How do a university's challenges—budget, enrollment, faculty recruitment, image—relate to the intended change?

In any organization, many forces contribute to maintaining the status quo. The academic leader in one Partnership project knew that none of the health sciences faculties at his institution wanted curricular change. To prevent that resistance from being an impediment to change, he considered both the sources of the departments' funds and their size and then created ad hoc extradepartmental, cross-college curriculum committees involving faculty who wanted to move toward change. In most cases, members of these new committees had been constrained by an established curriculum. Through their efforts, changes in curriculum were achieved by modifying courses without changing course requirements, changing the teaching site of established courses from hospital to community locations, and creating new "elective" courses with the full intention that they would eventually be required.

Some of the most significant curricular changes were not regarded as formal "changes." For example, a course on health education that had focused on discharge planning became a course on prevention and health promotion when it moved to a community health center. A course that introduced clinical skills to students as they examined hospital patients became an experience with relatively healthy people over a period of time when that course was relocated to a community-based site. By knowing the power configuration and attitudes toward the intended change, this leader created alternative structures to support change.

• *Build a team to carry out educational reform.* Individual leaders need influential allies—like-minded members of a leadership team—to initiate and sustain organizational adaptation on this scale. A team can carry reform forward at multiple levels within the organization when the person in a leadership position—a dean, for example—moves on. And a core group committed to the success of the reform can sustain efforts over the long interval required to adapt complex systems.

The leader of one Partnership project—a medical dean and vice president for health affairs—created a leadership team from the beginning. Initially, the team was made up of like-minded academics, but before long it was expanded to include community members. Now the team manages the project collectively: each team member is responsible for seeing to it that his or her respective constituency remains involved.

The leadership team has developed "rules" for engagement of larger groups of stakeholders, and those rules are nonnegotiable. Decisions related to the Partnership—decisions about the budget process, position papers, retreats—are evaluated in terms of the overall objectives of the Partnership. The stated objectives of the partnership have become the principles or "rules" that guide the leadership team. Now the ownership of the reform ideas reaches far beyond the original executive team. In fact, the membership of the executive team has changed over time. But the reforms—and the original rules that defined their development—continue.

• *Resist the inclination to deliberate further.* Considering the possible impact of change and anticipating the logistical consequences is always prudent and necessary. But *all* the doubts, questions, and uncertainties of a proposed change will never be resolved. Curriculum committees may recommend detailed planning. Faculty groups may advocate complex systems of student assessment. But leaders need to recognize that these approaches often limit creativity and inhibit reasoned judgment about the overall process. Although people in academic health centers will often urge more study, more time for planning, more consideration of the effects of change, prolonging the deliberative process can contribute to failure. Leaders need to strike a balance between thoughtful consideration of the proposed changes and the need to act in a timely manner.

Following many months of preparation, a status report on curriculum was presented to the board of one of the Community Partnerships projects by each of three different schools associated with that project. After listening to all three presentations, one community representative asked, "Why is it taking you so long?" At another Partnership site, when an evaluator described how evaluation would measure student performance against established curricular outcomes when implemented, another community member posed the same question: "Why is it taking so long?"

Deliberation is a characteristic of the faculty of academe—a tactic to delay or scuttle or both. For the members of any organization, the known is always more comfortable than the unknown. For academe participating in Community Partnerships, hospitals, and their cultures represent the known. Communities and the people who live in them—their schools, churches, and families—represent the unknown. In many cases, the prolonged deliberation that is characteristic of academe is a function of discomfort with new situations. While it must be understood and dealt with, it cannot be allowed to impede worthy change.

- *Begin early to modify the faculty reward system.* Leaders of health professions educational change need to pursue the development of faculty reward criteria consistent with the intended change very early in the change process. Promotion and tenure are the rewards of research (generally) and scholarship (sometimes) in the current system. To be community-focused in scholarship is to be no less scholarly, but the presumption that the highest level of scholarship can be identified only by the quantity of published articles, for example, may discourage talented assistant professors from devoting their careers to important community-responsive longitudinal research. If educational reform is to be successful, the definition of scholarship within an institution must be expanded to encompass the work of faculty conducting community-responsive research.

Time and again faculty—especially assistant professors—have been put at career risk by committing to the Community Partnerships initiative. The faculty and academic leaders in the Community Partnerships have had to choose between doing the work that would contribute to career advancement and doing the work of the institution in linking with communities and educating students. They have been faced with the incongruity between the goals of the Partnership and their institution's reward structure.

In one case, an extraordinarily capable physician teacher felt that he had to put his participation in the Partnership on hold while he acted on the advice of his dean and department head and took the actions necessary to get promoted. In another case, the director of one of the medical programs involved in a Partnership had to produce "outcome measures" for promotion rather than do scholarly work directly associated with the Partnership.

Yet there are positive examples as well—faculty who have been promoted *because* of their work with Community Partnerships. In such cases, promotion and tenure rules have been adapted by the institution so that they are consistent with the intentions of the Community Partnerships initiative. In effect, institutions are adapting and, in doing so, lending the weight of a powerful reward structure to the goal of sustaining educational change.

Communities

Through the Community Partnerships initiative, we have learned that we do ourselves—and communities—no favor by romanticizing the construct of *community*. Communities in general are an amalgam of frequently warring factions, with hostilities fueled by rumor. The Partnership communities are no different. The Community Partnerships are often seen as one more source of money— a commodity to argue over and seek to control. Even in the smallest rural communities, multiple factions—doctors, nurses, the hospital, community health centers, the local health department, nursing homes, child welfare agencies, public schools, and citizen advocacy groups—seek to preserve their reason for being by enhancing their resource base. In larger cities, neighborhoods function the same way. The politics of survival and control is basic to community organizations of all sizes.

To communities, health professions education is a means to an end—a concept that academic leaders often have great difficulty grasping. Communities are content to let universities educate their professionals, but they want institutions to listen: communities want appropriate care they can afford, they want to be respected, and they want the institutions that serve them—local government and hospitals as well as universities—to be responsive to the needs they identify.

Although communities do not necessarily share a dean's or department head's view of the primacy of health professions education, community members *are* willing to assume a role in the process of educating future providers. Their motivation for willingness to participate is different than academic leaders might assume: communities relate health professions training to local needs and services, and they link participation to more and better health care for their area and expanded options for their children. But communities, by participating, serve more than their own interests; they have much to teach health professionals and academic leaders.

Community representatives have a very strong influence on the reform of health professions institutions. More often than not, these people make personal and organizational sacrifices to ensure the success of their Community Partnership. In one Partnership, citizens raised their voices and marshaled their resources to help the community's children. They gave physical space in school buildings where there was little room to spare. They allocated tax revenues to build new buildings. They called attention to problems as they are lived—without the boundaries imposed by professionals.

Through the Community Partnerships, communities have shown a willingness to commit to the long-term goal of more primary care providers to benefit their neighborhoods and towns. They have shown a willingness to risk being "used," as they put it, by academics—those who study community "problems," publish articles based on their studies (often getting promoted as a result), yet have little impact on the problems themselves. Communities are willing to risk a great deal to get what they need in the long run.

To lead educational reform, leaders need to appreciate and promote the strengths communities can bring to health professions education. Leaders need to understand the nature of communities and work within that understanding. Academic leaders need to put aside preconceptions about community limitations and seek to build effective coalitions based on mutual interest and respect. When working with communities, leaders need to be mindful of these lessons:

• *Communities' stake in health professions education needs to be valued and cultivated.* To build on communities' motivation for change in health professions education, leaders must understand their needs and desires and respect their strengths. For communities, trust is the main ingredient of a successful relationship. When working to build coalitions to support community-based health professions education, leaders need to commit time to the process and be patient in seeking results. Communities are complex relational networks developed over many years. No leader can expect to develop trusting relationships with these networks quickly. In fact, to be in a hurry is to be counterproductive. Interaction, mutual interest, honesty, and respect—the factors that foster trust in a working relationship—must be present in community relationships.

• *Barriers to collaboration must be broken down.* Some barriers to collaboration are real—a function of institutions and their structures. Other barriers are perception-based, but they are no less real to those who believe in them. Leaders need to identify barriers to collaboration between institutions and communities—both real and perceived—and systematically dismantle them. Community members, for example, tend to be in awe of deans and others who have attained prestige within institutions. But if this "awe" prevents appropriate interaction between a community and an institution, it is a barrier. A community representative serving on the board of one of the Community Partnerships says that she would not have considered calling the medical school dean, who was also a member, during the early months of the Partnership. After a number of meetings and conversations, however, she came to realize that a phone call was not only acceptable but necessary to conduct the business of the Partnership.

Leaders interested in successfully linking with communities need to understand the personal sacrifice that participation may require of community members. While institutional representatives are generally paid for the time they expend on meetings, community participants are often volunteers missing work, skipping a lunch break, or scrambling to find someone to sit with the kids so they can attend a meeting during business hours. Whenever possible, leaders must seek to keep these very real demands from becoming a barrier to community involvement.

Jargon and complex managerial processes may also represent barriers to community participation and trust. Curriculum decision making, behavioral objectives, and strategic planning are not part of the culture of communities. Modifying language and sharing information about systems may support ongoing community involvement. Breaking down such barriers between community participants and academe strengthens collaborative efforts.

• *Communities need to be given the opportunity to define themselves.* Communities, as was stated in Chapter Six, are more than areas contained within boundaries on a map. They are collections of diverse groups, formed and reformed by common issues and history. Business and industry, schools, providers, and interest groups all have a part in community. Individual representatives of an institution cannot easily define community; efforts to do so have often been counterproductive. To engage communities in the process of redirecting health professions education, leaders need to be open enough to let communities define themselves over the course of the project.

Such definition and redefinition can be troublesome to those who like things neat and predictable. But "neat" and "predictable" are not characteristics generally common to communities. People move in and out of communities, and with new arrivals come new languages, cultures, and challenges. Using a community college district as the definition of community worked for a few months in one Community Partnership. Before long, however, the Partnership discovered that important health and human services were being provided in a town outside the district. Under the circumstances, the Partnership had to redefine the community. An ever-changing definition of community begs the question, Who represents community? The answer has been dynamic to date and will continue to be so. Communities must be given the space to define themselves, however messy that may be for academics.

Building New Organizational Structures

If organizational leaders lack the power to achieve major change on their own, coalitions built to create linking organizational structures between communities and institutions often provide the needed foundation for change. These new structures are responsible for creating and sustaining academic community health systems for the purpose of educating health professionals. Creating a new organizational structure, then, is one of the most important activities for a leader interested in achieving change.

As discussed in Chapter Seven, building a new organization is not easy. Even among the Community Partnerships, some formed organizations only to comply with the design of the initiative. But for a majority of the Partnerships, building and maintaining a strong linking organization has been primary to the success of the project. Leaders building organizational structures to support change may wish to draw on the lessons these Partnerships have learned:

• *Good leaders find and develop other leaders.* While academic leaders are important, they are not sufficient to ensure the success of a new organizational structure. Capable leaders from community health centers, the provider community, civic organizations, and medical, nursing, and other health professions schools are basic to the success of a new structure. They bring differing perspectives and constituencies into the process. Good leaders seek allies—from within their own organizations as well as outside it—and draw those allies into the process.

Within academic institutions, a vice president for health affairs, a provost, or a president may bring a broader view to the work of the new organizational structure. In several Partnerships, the university president was brought successfully into the initiative. In the majority of those instances, the president's view of the direction for the institution was consistent with that of the Community Partnerships initiative. In fact, as these presidents learned more about

Partnerships, they generally saw them as an effective means of operationalizing their own direction for their institution.

The examples are many, but the theme tends to be the same—finding ways to link the expertise of universities to the solution of local problems and to make universities more relevant to their founders' intentions. In public and private institutions, presidents have sought to increase access to higher education, spark economic development, or return to land-grant institutional roots through Partnership programs. Good leaders have found ways to bring others from academe into leadership roles to strengthen their Community Partnership.

Community health centers and provider networks must also be brought into the mix. The competition between academic health centers and community health centers can be very intense. Centers compete for patients, who represent profit in managed-care systems and income to faculty clinicians in fee-for-service arrangements. The dean leading one Community Partnership did not build in leadership roles for community health center directors in the Partnership's first two and one-half years. Over time, the project was impacted by the resulting distance between the dean and health center leadership. Although that situation may change in the future, generally speaking, the chances for successful reform are strengthened if reformers are able to find—and develop—leaders among community providers. Leaders from academe need to recognize the importance of sharing power with community health centers and other providers to build the leadership capacity of the new organization. If leaders from these key areas do not emerge, they must be cultivated. A new linking structure must be built on the diverse skills of the each Partnership's collective leadership.

• *Boards must balance competing interests.* One of the major intents of the Partnership structures is to enhance community involvement in decisions made about health professions education. Although academic institutions tend to play an important role in the work of the Partnerships, given their expertise and control over the educational process, it is critical that neither community nor academe dominate the Partnership organization. Each individual who serves on the Partnership board, for example, must strive to see the new linking organization as separate from the interests of either academe or community.

In one instance, a community leader prevented nursing students from providing care to a neighborhood over which he claimed informal jurisdiction. As a result, people were denied needed care by their own representative. Whatever the personal opinions of the rest of the Partnership board, they chose not to challenge this person's claim. In another case, a community health center board member was interested only in the amount of grant money that would come to his budget under a subcontract. In reality, every Partnership has such dynamics.

Both institutional and community representatives must give up control to the new linking organizational structure in order to gain. Leaders must strive to balance the competing interests of Partnership organizations and work to ensure that no one influence becomes too prominent.

• *The new linking organization itself must have a vision.* New organizations must continually seek to define a vision—one that all participants recognize and affirm—to sustain long-term efforts. Because of the differing interests and perspectives of institutional and community representatives, new organizations will need to define, debate, discuss, and redefine the vision to make it "real" for all participants. This process, although time-consuming, is a critical part of the new linking organization's development. By continually defining a shared vision, members of the Partnership organization clarify their common intent, direction, and purpose—and renew their commitment to project goals.

The third and fourth years of the Community Partnerships might be accurately called the period of "vision discovery." All of the linking organizational structures—some successful and sustaining, some less successful—reexamined their purpose during this period. The events that triggered such analysis were many and varied. In two instances, for example, the departure of a leader led the board to consider its long-term purpose. In other cases, precipitating events were related to financial sustainability or involvement in other functions (such as graduate medical and nursing education, patient care, or high school career programs). In the early days, these organizations might have seen their sole purpose as securing Kellogg Foundation funding. With those funds diminishing and soon to be gone, however, these groups were faced with the need to examine their reason for being: *Why does the organization exist? Do the groups represented on the board need this organization? Why? What would be lost if the organization did not exist?* So far, the projects that appear to have the greatest chance for long-term sustainability have affirmed the need for the Partnership and recommitted to its purpose.

Public Policy

One of the most perplexing issues of the Community Partnerships initiative has been encouraging the projects to think about the public policy that both sustains the status quo and has the potential to encourage something new. Leaders of educational reform tend, as we all do, to think in terms of what is well known rather than what is less known. When thinking of "change," they tend to think in terms of adding courses to a curriculum, moving the context of a course, or redesigning student examinations. When leaders use this approach, some things will change, certainly, but much will remain unchanged. In the sense of the capacity of graduates to value, think, and act in new ways, little will be different. Comprehensive change is a systems issue—in this case, the health care delivery system. True educational reform is therefore an issue of public policy change.

As suggested earlier in this book, the policy-making process is confusing, frustrating, and distant. Until recently, money flowed to academic institutions without most academics needing to pay much attention to it or to its source; the money just came—the fruit of existing public policy.

Leaders of reform—whether from community, academic institutions, or Partnership organizations—do not routinely think about the public policy process either. But if institutions change in response to outside pressures, as the Community Partnerships model contends, the pressures of governmental agencies, licensure and accreditation bodies, and elected officials must be recognized and, where necessary, realigned.

Members of these groups influence governmental regulation and the allocation of public money. For every adaptation or new educational approach sought at the Partnership level, leaders must seek to inform policy makers of ways to strengthen public policy to support it. Because changes in the nature and location of health professions education will require changes in the way that education is governed and funded, leaders need to attend to the public policy arena throughout the change process.

- *Think about educational reform as a political process.* In the culture of academe, change is a data-influenced, rational process of moving from the status quo to something that has been proven to be better. But the status quo of health professions education has been shaped as much by public policy and funding as by rational deliberation. What people in communities want and need—and therefore what their elected officials want and need—must be addressed in this change process.

- *Think about the external environment from the very beginning.* Leaders of reform must identify potential allies outside of the institution very early in the process. Because communities at large, community representatives, and providers outside of academic health centers are less vested than insiders in maintaining the status quo, leaders often find it easier to identify external than internal allies.

As was stated earlier, no one leader can initiate and accomplish the desired level of change alone. Those who wish to lead change in health professions education must get to know the external environment and link with these "outsiders" from the beginning to form the basis for productive coalitions.

- *Declare success prematurely.* Effective leaders waste no time in declaring the success of their project as early as possible. They see to it that the reform is written about—even before many think there is anything to write about—and that the word gets out. Such declarations of success without hard data go against the grain of researchers, who traditionally take a scientific approach to disseminating "findings." But educational reform is not a scientific venture; it is a political one. The attention and visibility that declarations of success spawn tend to move projects closer to their desired goals.

- *Learn to speak the language of politics.* Most of us are isolated from the concerns of elected officials by our own professional expertise and organizational affiliation. The language each profession uses contributes to this isolation. School principals use the language of educators: they speak of objectives-based education, various acts and public laws, cooperative education, and scores on state and national examinations. Hospital administrators talk of occupancy rates, Medicaid expenditures, and Medicare regulations. Community health center administrators speak of WIC programs, FQHCs, and 330 clinics. Social workers talk of foster care, in-home treatment, and group facilitation. Nurse educators speak of advanced-practice nurses, clients, prescriptive privileges, and scope of practice. Doctors talk of physician extenders.

Such is the language of providers—a language that isolates. But policy makers speak the language of politics. Policy makers want to know how much care can be provided, by whom, and at what cost. They are concerned about jobs, taxes, health care, and other aspects of the quality of life. In years past, public tax money flowed conveniently to human service agencies, schools, and universities with few questions. Professionals and their organizations were able to remain isolated, both from people in communities and from the political process that supported their institutions. But as we have noted, if educational reform is to succeed, policy making can no longer be ignored. Leaders of reform must learn to speak the language of politics and relate their activities to the concerns of policy makers' constituencies.

Reflections for the Leader

Leaders of educational reform are important and they are not. Change requires individuals who will step forward with ideas about how things can be better, but individual leaders must give way to collective leadership—that intangible relational quality that links those who lead with those who follow. Leaders may have attributes that are essential to getting something started, but it is followers who accomplish change.

Leaders of reform in health professions education must work to create leadership to support change. They must build a team. They must transcend conventional boundaries and be willing to face their own inadequacies. In discussing transformational leadership, Burns (1978) called attention to the moral imperatives that may emerge when leaders and followers come together. Leaders who have mastered the art of creating leadership have discovered how to gain by giving away. The lessons true leaders have learned instruct all who would lead similarly:

- *Delegate the character of the educational reform to others.* Leaders who are marginally successful see the means and the end as one and the same. In their minds, neither is negotiable. But successful leaders are able to distinguish between *what* is to be done and *how* it is to be done. They turn their attention to the *what*—and often the *why*—and leave the *how* to others. They do not concern themselves with whether the new curriculum is integrated or problem-based, for example. They delegate the specifics of the educational reform, trusting that others who hold the vision will make the choices needed to accomplish the project's long-term goals.

- *Know what you want and be prepared to negotiate some of it away.* No matter how strongly an individual believes that all facets of a major reform are equally important, they are not. It is necessary, then, to know which elements are negotiable and which are not. Successful leaders of educational reform join with others in making this decision. Out of such a process of leaders working with followers, leadership emerges.

- *Be prepared to function on the edge.* Successful leaders are risk takers, unconcerned about the opinions of peers and about how their current job performance may impact future opportunities. Such individuals are prepared to do what is right, as determined collectively by leaders and followers. They do not follow a traditional career path (and do not care to). Job security is not their motivation. Unfortunately, a few leaders may discover that their success forces them to go elsewhere.

Three years into its funding period, one Community Partnership selected a new executive director to head the Partnership structure. Upon accepting the position, the individual declared, "I don't intend to be head of an organization that has only eighteen months left. This program will survive and grow. People need it." The power of this statement and the actions taken to back it up have been enough to ensure that the Partnership will indeed be around long after Kellogg Foundation funding has ended. In another case, however, a Partnership director left after three and one-half years of funding. On departing, he commented that "being in the middle— between community and academe—can be a lonely spot."

Leading health professions educational reform toward community *can* be a lonely job. In the beginning, at least, few are willing to help build a bridge between community and academe. If the building begins on the academic side, few academic colleagues are supportive; the approach is such a departure from the status quo that few seem to understand the potential. If the bridge building begins on the community side, suspicions about institutions abound. As one community leader remarked, "Why should we expect collaboration from either community organizations or from academe?" Building a bridge from the middle—in effect, from the new linking organization back to each side—is no less difficult or lonely. Leaders of new organizational structures have few, if any, colleagues in similar jobs. In this groundbreaking endeavor, there is no "career path."

In any circumstance, it is risky for a leader to give power and control away, placing his or her career in the hands of others. But that is the difference between assuming a position of authority (sometimes confused with being a leader) and true leadership. Ironically, there is really no choice: to successfully lead reform in health professions education, others must be involved. In spite of the ambiguity, power must be shared. To take another path—to maintain control—fundamentally alters the intent of the change and limits what leadership can accomplish.

Building Partnerships to Lead Reform

Woven throughout these observations has been considerable attention to both power and collaboration. Although the term *power* can evoke different meanings, depending on one's perspective, its use here is intended to be neutral—that is, carrying neither "good" nor "bad" associations. In this usage, *power* suggests a variety of reasons why people willingly (and sometimes unwillingly) do as others wish. Trust, respect for expertise, and influential connections may all be forms of power. As Lord Acton wrote, "Power tends to corrupt and absolute power corrupts absolutely." In a much later treatise, Rosabeth Kanter considered the leadership roles of women in organizations and offered a counterstatement: "Powerlessness corrupts and absolute powerlessness corrupts absolutely" (1977, p. 164). It is, in other words, counterproductive to ignore the role that power plays in leadership.

The relationship of the Partnership's organizational structure to universities and hospitals is a power relationship. The Community Partnerships' power, increasing in this changing health care

environment, is based on the capacity to affect the income of hospitals and their respective academic health centers—a function of
access to patients, some of whom will need to be admitted to one
hospital or another for care. In more than one Community Partnership, the tension is between community health centers' ability
to "hang together" and the hospitals' interest in splitting them
apart. For one Community Partnership with several community
health centers, reform of health professions education toward out-
of-hospital experiences requires the centers to cast their lot together
rather than separately. This coalition among community health
centers is the Partnership's source of power. In other Partnerships
with access to additional out-of-hospital sites (such as school-based
clinics), the coalition of schools becomes the power base.

Communities have power as well. In many cases, that power is
based on the capacity of community representatives to influence
state appropriation to higher education. In two of the Partnerships,
the communities have gained sufficient knowledge and commitment to act on their own behalf. The communities know that they
need more primary care, and they know the educational and legislative systems that affect its availability. To get what they need,
community representatives in this Partnership have connected with
state legislators. Universities cannot now ignore their communities
without risking state appropriations.

It is equally counterproductive to ignore collaboration. Leaders
of educational reform must build coalitions and work from the outside in, as has been noted. The issue for these leaders becomes how
to collaborate with an eye to the dynamics of academic health centers, the nature of communities, the needs of the new linking structures, and the demands of the public policy arena. It has been
suggested that building functional, sustainable coalitions requires
not only the work of a leader; it requires leadership.

We do not know very much about the sort of leadership required
for educational reform. The focus in the literature on leadership has
been too fixed on the attributes of leaders and managers, and on
their situations, for us to realize that the only way a person can be

declared a true leader is if others are prepared to follow. Leaders and followers, taken together, create leadership.

The Community Partnerships with Health Professions Education initiative is based on the premise that changing health professions education so that graduates are committed and responsive to people in communities requires both leaders and followers. It acknowledges that leaders can arise from anywhere—from academic health centers, from the provider community, from community health centers, from academic institutions, from community groups. To become leaders in this effort, representatives of hospitals, academic health centers, and other institutions of professional expertise need to admit what they do not know. Deans and university representatives must realize that the *authority* vested in a position is not leadership—especially when those representatives are working with consumers and the provider institutions that make up a community. The right to lead is granted by those who follow.

For community representatives, the same is true. A position in local government, in the school system, in a hospital, or in a community health center does not, in and of itself, make an individual a leader. Formal authority does not create leadership. In either case, building functional, sustainable coalitions requires *all* to give in order to gain.

As has been stated, building coalitions is hard work, and it takes a long time. Whether we come from the community or from academe, we know that sharing power and control is very difficult. Early in the life of one Community Partnership, an academic leader gave control of the Partnership budget to the newly established community/university board. To facilitate the budget process, the academic leader held two all-day sessions (on Saturdays at a community site) to answer community members' budget questions. Over the course of the sessions, two things became clear to the participants: the university leader was prepared to answer every question asked (What's an FTE faculty member? If 25 percent of a faculty member's time is to be paid from this budget, what does the person do with the other 75 percent? and so on), and the university leader really did not intend to control the nature of the final budget. In the end, the community decided to follow this dean. He helped create a collaboration with the potential followers, and they followed. The project moved from the work of an individual leader to *leadership*.

As is the case in every effective Partnership, building collaboration between academe and community works both ways. Sometimes the community creates the opportunity for leadership to emerge. Communities, which want physicians and nurses to come to their towns and stay, call it "recruitment and retention." They provide land and physical facilities; they contribute tax money and housing for students; they conduct celebrations of their distinctiveness for students to experience. People in communities ask to see "my nurse" or "my doctor" even when they know very well that both are students; they attend student graduations. With a little bit of support from academic leadership, communities make uncompromising commitments and create opportunities for the generally more skeptical faculty of medical and nursing schools.

Giving up control—control over ideas, problem definitions, solutions, budgets, meeting agendas, priorities, even long-term vision—is exceedingly difficult. The necessary reflection on each person's individual need for control is profound. Each person committed to a partnership between communities and institutions must be able to return to the organization or group he or she represents knowing that interest in control remains a prime motivator in those environments.

It is not necessary to choose between power and collaboration; one is not the antithesis of the other. Too often we make the mistake of forcing a choice even when both are necessary for success. Among the Community Partnerships, both power and collaboration are needed to achieve educational reform. Power is critical, but it must be given away by all parties to the new organizational structure—and then used wisely. That process is complex, difficult, and rare, but that is leadership.

Resources

• •

Alliance for Health Reform
1133 Twentieth Street NW, Suite 220
Washington, D.C. 20036
p 202/466–5626

American Academy of Family Physicians
8880 Ward Parkway
Kansas City, MO 64114
p 816/333–9700
f 816/333–9855

American Academy of Pediatrics
141 NW Point Boulevard
Elk Grove, IL 60009
p 708/228–5005
f 708/228–5097

American Academy of Physicians Assistants
950 North Washington Street
Alexandria, VA 22314
p 703/836–2272
f 703/684–1924

American Association of Colleges of Nursing
One Dupont Circle, Suite 530
Washington, D.C. 20036
p 202/463–6930
f 202/785–8320

American College of Osteopathic Family Physicians
330 East Algonquin Road, Suite One
Arlington Heights, IL 60005
p 800/323–0794
f 708/228–9755

American College of Physicians
Independence Mall West
6th at Race
Philadelphia, PA 19106
p 215/351–2400
f 215/351–2594

American Medical Student Association
1890 Preston White Drive
Reston, VA 22091
p 703/620–6600
f 703/620–5873

Association of American Medical Colleges
2450 N Street NW
Washington, D.C. 20037
p 202/828–0408
f 202/828–1125

Association of Minority Health Professions Schools
711 Second Street NE, Suite 200
Washington, D.C. 20002

p 202/544–7499
f 202/546–7105

Association of Professors of Medicine
1101 Connecticut Avenue, Suite 700
Washington, D.C. 20036
p 202/857–1158
f 202/223–4579

Association of Program Directors in Internal Medicine
700 Thirteenth Street NW, Suite 250
Washington, D.C. 20005
p 800/622–4558
f 202/393–1658

Association of Schools of Public Health
1660 L Street NW, Suite 204
Washington, D.C. 20036
p 202/296–1099
f 202/296–1252

Council on Graduate Medical Education
Division of Medicine, Bureau of Health Professions, HRSA
Parklawn Building
5600 Fishers Lane
Rockville, MD 20857
p 301/443–6190
f 301/443–8890

The Robert Wood Johnson Foundation
College Road
P.O. Box 2316
Princeton, NJ 08543–2316
p 609/452-8701

Health of the Public
National Program Office
University of California, San Francisco
San Francisco, CA 94143–0994
p 415/476–8907
f 415/476–3429

Available publications include "Academic Health Centers and the
Community: A Practical Guide for Creating Shared Visions,"
Arthur Kaufman and Robert E. Waterman (eds.), "Health of the
Public: A Challenge to Academic Health Centers. Strategies for
Reorienting Academic Health Centers Toward Community Needs."

W.K. Kellogg Foundation
One Michigan Avenue East
Battle Creek, MI 49017–4058
p 616/968–1611
f 616/968–0413

Available publications include "Community Partnerships: A Kellogg Initiative in Health Professions Education," "Community Partnerships: Graduate Medical and Nursing Education," "The Doctor
Track," "A Primary Care Primer," and "What the Public Values in
Its Health Care System: A National Opinion Survey."

National Association of Community Health Centers
1330 New Hampshire Avenue NW, Suite 122
Washington, D.C. 20036
p 202/659–8008
f 202/659–8519

Available publications include "Teaching Community Health
Centers."

National Association of County Health Officials
440 First Street NW, Suite 500
Washington, D.C. 20001
p 202/783–5550
f 202/783–1583

National Health Policy Forum
2021 K Street NW, Suite 800
Washington, D.C. 20052
p 202/872–1390
f 202/785–0114

Available publications include "Health Professions Training in Ambulatory Settings: Turning Talk into Action."

Pew Health Professions Commission
Center for Health Professions
1388 Sutter Street, Suite 805
San Francisco, CA 94109
p 415/476–8181
f 415/476–4113

Available publications include "Contemporary Issues in Health Professions Education and Workforce Reform," "Health Professions Education and Relationship-Centered Care," "Interdisciplinary Collaborative Teams in Primary Care: A Model Curriculum and Resource Guide," and "Resource Book for Health Professions Education Strategic Planning."

Society of Teachers of Family Medicine
8880 Ward Parkway
Kansas City, MO 64114
p 816/333–9700
f 816/333–3884

References

Abbott, A. *The System of Professions: An Essay on the Division of Labor.* Chicago: University of Chicago Press, 1988.

Alliance for Health Reform. "The Doctor Track." Washington, D.C.: Alliance for Health Reform, 1994.

Association of American Medical Colleges Questionnaire. (1990).

Baldridge, J. V., and Deal T. E. *Managing Change in Educational Organizations.* Berkeley, Calif.: McCutchan, 1975.

Bland, C. J., Meurer, L. N., and Maldonado, G. "Determinants of Primary Care Specialty Choice." Report prepared for Future Directions for Research in Primary Health Care, University of Minnesota, Aug. 23, 1994.

Bland, C. J., Starnaman, S., Zonia, S., and Rosenberg, L. "Institutional Factors Likely to Relate to the Successful Implementation of the Community Partnership Projects." Report prepared for the W.K. Kellogg Foundation, Battle Creek, Mich., 1992.

Bledstein, B. J. *The Culture of Professionalism: The Middle Class and the Development of Higher Education in America.* New York: W.W. Norton, 1976.

Blendon, R. J., and Altman, D. E. "Kaiser Health Reform Project: Kaiser/Harvard/PRSA Survey of Public Knowledge." Menlo Park, Calif.: Henry J. Kaiser Family Foundation, Oct. 1993.

Blendon, R. J., Brodie, M., Hyams, T. S., and Benson, J. M. "The American Public and the Critical Choices for Health System Reform." *Journal of the American Medical Association*, 1994, *271*(19), 1539–1544.

Bloom, S. W. "Structure and Ideology in Medical Education: An Analysis of Resistance to Change." *Journal of Health and Social Behavior*, 1988, (29), 294–306.

Boex, J. R. "Primary Care Practitioner: Analyses of Competencies, Costs, and Quality of Care and Effects of Training on Supply." Report prepared for the W.K. Kellogg Foundation, Battle Creek, Mich., Aug. 1993.

Boland, P. "Market Overview and Delivery System Dynamics." In P. Boland, *Making Managed Health Care Work: A Practical Guide to Strategies and Solutions*. Gaithersburg, Md.: Aspen, 1993.

Boyer, E. *Scholarship Reconsidered: Priorities of the Professoriate*. Princeton, N.J.: Carnegie Foundation for the Advancement of Teaching, 1990.

Brody, H., and others. "The Mammalian Medical Center for the 21st Century." *Journal of the American Medical Association*, 1993, *270*(9), 1097–1100.

Bucher, R., and Stelling, J. "Four Characteristics of Professional Organizations." In R. L. Blankenship (ed.), *Colleagues in Organizations*. New York: Wiley, 1977.

Burns, J. M. *Leadership*. New York: HarperCollins, 1978.

Cohen, J. J. *AAMC Reporter*. Washington, D.C.: Association of American Medical Colleges, 1994a.

Cohen, J. J. "Finding the Silver Lining Without the Golden Eggs." Paper presented at the 105th annual meeting of the Association of American Medical Colleges, Boston, Oct. 1994b.

Cowill, J. M. "Recommendations to Improve Health Care Access, Cost, and Quality Through Physician Workforce Reform." Statement of the Council on Graduate Medical Education before the Senate Finance Committee of the U.S. Senate, Mar. 8, 1994.

Crossen, C. *Tainted Truths*. New York: Simon & Schuster, 1994.

Dewar, T. "Community Partnerships Seminar Three." Paper presented at a networking meeting sponsored by the W.K. Kellogg Foundation, Durham, N.H., July 1990.

Dobson, A., Coleman, K., and Mechanic, R. "Analysis of Teaching Hospital Costs." Fairfax, Va.: Lewin-VHI, Aug. 10, 1994.

Donaldson, M., Yordy, K., and Vanselow, N. (eds.). "Defining Primary Care: An Interim Report." Report of the Committee on the Future of Primary Care, Division of Health Care Services, Institute of Medicine. Washington, D.C.: National Academy Press, 1994.

Etzioni, A. *A Comparative Analysis of Complex Organizations*. New York: Free Press, 1961.

"Fourth Report to Congress and the Department of Health and Human Services Secretary." Report prepared for the U.S. Department of Health and Human Services, Washington, D.C., Jan. 1994.

Garg, M. L., Boex, J. R., Davis, C. K., and Rodos, J. J. "Reforming Graduate

Medical Education Financing to Promote Primary Care and Community-Based Training." Report prepared for the W.K. Kellogg Foundation, Battle Creek, Mich., 1993.

Ginzberg, E. *The Medical Triangle*. Cambridge, Mass.: Harvard University Press, 1990.

Grace, H. "Views from the Tugboat." Paper presented at the Community Partnerships Leadership and Model Development Seminar, Indianapolis, Oct. 1990.

Graduate Medical Education National Advisory Committee. *Report to the Advisory Committee to the Secretary, Department of Health and Human Services*. Washington, D.C.: Government Printing Office, 1980.

Henderson, T. M. *State Efforts to Increase Community-Based Medical Education*. Washington, D.C.: George Washington University Press, 1994.

Honan, W. H. "Academic Disciplines Increasingly Entwine, Recasting Scholarship." *New York Times*, Mar. 3, 1994, p. A19.

Howe, J. P., Osterweis, M., and Rubin, E. R. (eds.). *Academic Health Centers: Missions, Markets, and Paradigms for the Next Century*. Washington, D.C.: Association of Academic Health Centers, 1994.

Jolly, P., and Hudley, D. M. *AAMC Date Book*. Washington, D.C.: Association of American Medical Colleges, 1994.

Kanter, R. M. *The Change Masters*. New York: Simon & Schuster, 1984.

Kanter, R. M. *Men and Women of the Corporation*. New York: Basic Books, 1977.

Kassenbaum, D. G., and Szenas, P. L. "Specialty Preference of Graduating Medical Students: 1992 Update." *Academic Medicine*, 1992, 67(11), 800–806.

Knott, J. H. "Kellogg Community Partnerships Cluster Evaluation: Public Policy Arena." Paper presented at a networking meeting sponsored by the W.K. Kellogg Foundation, Johnson City, Tenn., Oct. 1994.

Kosterlitz, J. "The Spoils of Reform." *National Journal*, Aug. 20, 1994, pp. 1970–1974.

Lee, P. R., and Brindis, C. D. "Public Policy Issues Affecting the Health Care Delivery System of Adolescents." *Journal of Adolescent Health Care*, 1990 11(5), 387–397.

McKnight, J. "The Need for Oldness." Paper presented at the Center on Aging, McGaw Medical Center, Northwestern University, Evanston, Ill., Fall 1986.

Maslow, A. H. *Motivation and Personality*. New York: HarperCollins, 1954.

Matherlee, K. R. "Federal Support of Medical Education: Framing the Issues for the Systems Reform Debate." Issue brief no. 648. Washington, D.C.: National Health Policy Forum, George Washington University, 1994.

Moore, G. T. "The Impact of Managed Care on the Medical Education Environment." Report prepared for the Bureau of Health Professions, Health Resources and Services Administration, U.S. Department of Health and Human Services, Nov. 1993.

Nix, H. L. "Concepts of Community and Community Leadership." In W. R. Lassey and M. Sashkin (eds.), *Leadership and Social Change*. San Diego, Calif.: University Associates, 1983.

O'Neill T. *All Politics Is Local: And Other Rules of the Game* (pp. xv–xvi). New York: Times Books, 1994.

Pew Health Professions Commission. "Healthy America: Practitioners for 2005." October 1991.

Politzer, R. M., Harris, D. L., Gaston, M. H., and Mullan, F. "Primary Care Physician Supply and the Medically Underserved." *Journal of the American Medical Association*, 1991, *266*(1), 104–109.

Reinhardt, U. E. "Planning the Nation's Health Workforce: Let the Market In." *Inquiry*, 1994, *31*, 250–263.

Rivo, M. L., and Satcher, D. "Improving Access to Health Care Through Physician Workforce Reform." *Journal of the American Medical Association*, 1993, *270*(9), 1074–1078.

Rost, J. C. *Leadership for the Twenty-First Century*. Westport, Conn.: Praeger, 1991.

Schön, D. *The Reflective Practitioner*. New York: Basic Books, 1983.

Shaddish, W. R., Cook, T. D., and Leviton, L. C. *Foundations of Program Evaluation: Theories of Practice*. Newbury Park, Calif.: Sage, 1991.

Size, T. "Managing Partnerships: The Perspective of a Rural Hospital Cooperative." *Health Care Management Review*, 1993, *18*(1), 31–41.

Solloway, M., Weiss, K., and Fagan, M. J. *A Chartbook on the Supply, Training, and Distribution of Physicians*. Washington, D.C.: George Washington University Center for Health Policy Research, 1994.

Taub, R. P. "Nuance in Meaning and Evaluation: Finding Community and Development." Paper presented at the Research Conference, May 5, 1989, The New School, New York.

Tinder, G. *Community: Reflections on a Tragic Ideal*. Baton Rouge: Louisiana State University Press, 1980.

Treadwell, H. Remarks presented at the Community Partnerships Fellows Seminar, Rockland, Maine, Aug. 1994.

Weiner, J. "Assessing the Impact of Managed Care on the U.S. Physician Workforce." Report prepared for the Bureau of Health Professions, Health

Resources and Services Administration, U.S. Department of Health and Human Services, U.S. Department of Commerce: National Technical Information Services, PB94–142288, Nov. 1993.

Weiner, J. P. "Forecasting the Effects of Health Reform on U.S. Physician Work-force Requirement," *Journal of the American Medical Association*, *272*(3), July 20, 1994, 222–230.

Wilson, M. P., and others. *Handbook of Health Professions Education: Responding to New Realities in Medicine, Dentistry, Pharmacy, Nursing, Allied Health, and Public Health*. San Francisco: Jossey-Bass, 1983.

Wofford, H. *Of Kennedy and Kings*. Pittsburgh, Penn.: University of Pittsburgh Press, 1980.

World Federation for Medical Education. *Edinburgh Declaration: World Federation for Medical Education Report*. Edinburgh, U.K.: World Federation for Medical Education, Aug. 7–12, 1988.

Yankelovich, D. "How Public Opinion Really Works." *Fortune*, Oct. 5, 1992, pp. 102–108.

Index